# 13 Is the New 18

# Is the New 18

*And other things my children taught me
while I was having a nervous breakdown
being their mother*

# Beth J. Harpaz

*Crown Publishers*

NEW YORK

Some names and identifying details have been changed.

Library of Congress Cataloging-in-Publication Data

Harpaz, Beth J.
13 is the new 18—and other things my children taught me
while I was having a nervous breakdown being their mother /
Beth J. Harpaz.—1st ed.
p.    cm.
1. Parenting—Humor.    2. Parent and teenager—Humor.
I. Title.    II. Title: Thirteen is the new eighteen.
PN6231.P2H37 2009
306.87402'07—dc22    2008016547
ISBN 978-0-307-39641-9

Printed in the United States of America

Design by Robert C. Olsson

10  9  8  7  6  5  4  3  2  1

First Edition

*This book is dedicated to my boys*

# Contents

PROLOGUE: A LETTER TO THE READER    1

*1*   Unjumpable Son   5

*2*   Are We There Yet?   20

*3*   Your Boxers Are Showing   42

*4*   Consulting the Experts   69

*5*   Another Call from School   94

*6*   The Eighth-Grade Prom   113

*7*   Contraband   138

*8*   The Mysteries of Girls   161

*9*   Epiphanies   187

*10*   The Secret Lives of Teenagers   211

*11*   Getting to Know You   226

*12*   Good-bye Thirteen, Hello Fourteen, Hello Hope   239

*13*   Meditations on the Past and Future   257

ACKNOWLEDGMENTS   273

# *13 Is the New 18*

# A LETTER TO THE READER

*Dear Reader,*

If your child has already turned eight, nine, or ten, then you've long been done with diapers, bottles, and sippy cups, toilet training and tantrums. By now your child can read and multiply, swim and ride a two-wheeler, and manage OK without you in most everyday tasks.

The highlights of your child's life are simple, but wonderful in their simplicity: scoring a goal in soccer. Staying up late on a sleepover. Being tall enough to ride a big roller coaster. Seeing a movie the day it opens. Pigging out on Halloween candy. Winning at Monopoly. Blowing a perfect bubble with a piece of gum.

And while it's only recently that your child has stopped believing in Santa and the Tooth Fairy, he's young enough that deep down inside, he still holds on to a shred of hope that they might actually be real. He just doesn't want to admit it.

Enjoy this time, dear reader. Because soon your golden child will turn eleven, twelve . . . and then thirteen. And then one day, all of a sudden, none of those things that used to make him happy will matter.

He will grow tall in the night and nothing will fit in the morning. Strange smells will emanate from his shoes, his body, and his room. He will get in trouble and people will blame you. He will admire celebrities who scare you. You will find yourself screaming things your mother screamed at you, and he will tune you out with ear buds and tiny glowing screens. You've been dreaming of the day, ever since he was born, that he would allow you to sleep past dawn, but now it will take a bagpipe band to rouse him before lunch.

He will have nothing but disdain for Santa and the Tooth Fairy, but he will believe that you are obligated to provide presents and money whenever he asks, and he will be outraged when you say no. He will spend huge sums of cash on things you don't understand, like texting and downloading music, and if you should ever read those text messages or hear those songs, you will want to kill yourself. And his sneakers will cost more than your first semester of college.

He may also do dangerous things, stupid things, and possibly even illegal things. And even if he isn't doing them, you will drive yourself insane wondering if he is. He will abhor the sound of your voice, the sight of your face, and the ways of your family, which used to be his family, before he decided to pretend that he is no longer related to you. From now on, in fact, he will do everything he can to avoid you, including gluing his cell phone to his ear, but not answering it when you call.

Perhaps you think of yourself as someone who has kept up with trends, who is not out of touch despite the fact that you were born sometime in the last century and now spend a ridiculous amount of time trying to hide that roll of fat around your waist and your gray hair (or lack of hair).

Your own parents probably grew up during the Great Depression or World War II, so it was no surprise that there was a generation gap when you were a teenager. But you never anticipated you would have a generation gap with your own child.

After all, you listened to music with degenerate lyrics! You drank before you were legally old enough! Maybe you even smoked pot and had what is almost never referred to these days as premarital sex. Not that you want your child to do any of these things before, say, the age of twenty-nine, but maybe you thought you could use your accumulated wisdom to do a better job understanding and guiding your teenager than your parents did with you.

Well, as a parent, you may still be useful for a few things, like doing the laundry and providing transportation. But other than that, to a thirteen-year-old, you are nothing but old and old-fashioned. Your accumulated wisdom is boring; your efforts to keep up with technology are a joke; and even your wardrobe is embarrassing.

## Prologue

Does all this scare you? It should. Read on, and hear my story. You see, dear reader, things have changed since you were thirteen. Childhood doesn't fade away with the onset of puberty; now it disappears all at once. Thirteen is the new eighteen, and nothing in your own adolescence can prepare you for this moment. Soon you will be the shortest person in your house and your taste in music will be despised. That kid who just a few years ago wouldn't leave you alone long enough to drink a cup of coffee before it got cold now can't bear to spend five minutes in your presence.

But there's nothing you can do about any of this, so accept your fate. Get your own iPod, beg your kid to help you download some Bruce Springsteen, and try to find the humor in it all.

*Sincerely,*
*The Mother of Taz*

# UNJUMPABLE SON

*T*he phone rings. My husband, Elon, answers it.

"It's a girl!" he says, sounding panicky.

We have two sons, and if it's a girl, then it must be for Taz, the one who's just turned thirteen. His little brother, Sport, is only eight, and doesn't yet acknowledge that girls exist.

"Taz, phone!" I yell down the hall toward his room.

Taz comes out and takes the receiver from his father. "Hello? Oh hi, Greg."

I look at Elon. "Greg is not a girl," I say.

"OK," he says. "I didn't know."

It's an honest mistake. You see, thirteen-year-old boys come in two distinct sizes: little ones who sound like they swallowed helium, and big ones with low voices who can empty a crowded room just by removing one enormous, smelly sneaker.

The phone call was from one of the little ones, but our son is one of the big ones. He wears size-eleven sneakers, curses like a rapper, and inhales a foot-long sandwich in four bites. When you call his cell phone, you get a message from before his voice got deep— a Munchkin-like "Yo, whaddup, it's Taz!"—but if he deigns to call you back, you think you're talking to Johnny Cash.

His tastes are surprisingly grown-up, too, considering that just a few months ago he thought he was living large if I allowed a bottle of soda in the house. But nowadays, his drink of choice isn't Coke. It's Starbucks Frappuccino.

"Coffee?" I shrieked when I first learned of his love of iced lattes and caramel macchiatos (whatever those are). "My thirteen-year-old is hooked on coffee?"

But then I remembered when I was in eighth grade, I took No-Doz to get through social studies class. (Ugh, those Federalist Papers were SOOOO boring!) If coffee had tasted as good then as it does now, I probably would have ditched the No-Doz for lattes, too.

Either way, Taz—like a lot of thirteen-year-olds—is a discriminating consumer. He likes salad, but only the baby spring mix. He likes sushi, but only cucumber rolls. (The thought of raw fish horrifies him.) And he likes spicy food—the more jalapeños, the better.

When I was a kid, I'd like to point out, spicy food did not exist (unless you count curried chicken in cream sauce, made from a recipe in *Ladies' Home Journal*). And the only place you could get Mexican food was Mexico. In contrast, Taz, like other kids who frequent Taco Bell or the local taqueria, knows the difference between burritos, tacos, tortillas, and quesadillas the way I knew my way around Fudgsicles, Creamsicles, and Eskimo Pies. It's no accident that Taz's namesake, the Tasmanian Devil cartoon character, is a teenage animal, known for his hearty appetite (not to mention his weakness for pretty Devil girls).

My Taz is also big on brands. He likes North Face. Timberland. Nike and Jordans. But knowing trademarks from generics is not just about clothes—it's about all kinds of products.

For example, one day when I'm headed to the drugstore, he asks me to buy Axe.

I am so proud of myself—I know what Axe is!

Well, actually another mom tipped me off—it's a deodorant popular among adolescent boys.

But I am not prepared for the ninety-nine varieties of Axe at the drugstore—row after row. They're all packaged in black dispensers with silver lettering, like some Vegas hotel room from the seventies. They have names like Adrenalin, Apollo, Phoenix, Kilo, and Tsunami. They come in body spray, deodorant sticks, shower gel. It's all very confusing to someone like me who has been buying the same brand of unscented Ban Roll-On since Ronald Reagan was in the White House.

At least I can rule out the aftershave (although a friend tells me that her son used aftershave for years before he actually started shaving). I shut my eyes and pull one can of Axe off the shelf, figuring that I am more likely to pick an acceptable scent by relying on the randomness of the universe than if I made a conscious decision based on what I think Taz will want, which would surely be wrong.

I hand my selection to the cashier without examining it too closely, pay for it, and keep the receipt in case I need to make an exchange. I bring it home, give it to Taz, and wait for the verdict.

"Is it OK?" I ask tentatively. "There were so many choices, I wasn't sure . . ."

Taz nods. "Thanks," he says. "Tsunami. This is good."

Hurray, I got the right kind of Axe! Even if it was sort of by accident. Maybe I'm not as out of touch as I had feared. I feel absurdly pleased with myself, the way I used to feel in high school if I happened to wear pink lip gloss or a velveteen blazer the same day that one of the Cool Girls did.

But now the rest of us—Elon, our youngest son, Sport, and I—have to live with the smell of Axe, and some days I'm not so sure it's any better than body odor. Taz uses it more than regularly, spraying not just his body but also his clothes and even his room.

It is a sickly sweet odor, strong and musky, like cheap incense, and it seeps out from under his closed door— his door is almost always closed—and into the hallway. There it creates a virtual mushroom cloud that eventually radiates into every corner of our small apartment. But the epicenter of the bomb zone is definitely traceable to his room.

"Ugh, I can't stand that smell," Elon says as he arrives home from work one day after a particularly powerful Axe detonation. Taz's room is right next to the front door, so eau de Axe always hits you hard the minute you step over the threshold. And when you first inhale it, you can't imagine how you're going to get on with your life, swallow your food, or concentrate on anything more complicated than watching TV.

"Don't worry," I tell Elon, "it's just the Axe. You'll get used to it. It's better than having our house smell like a locker room."

Indeed, as with most fumes that don't kill you, after a few minutes, your brain adjusts and it becomes less noticeable. Besides, it seems to have a half-life of about an hour. I suppose by then whatever was airborne has drifted to the floor, where we will absorb it through the soles of our feet for the rest of our lives. Come to think of it, maybe that's why Taz's sneakers don't smell quite as bad as some of his friends'.

But Elon insists that something more nefarious is going on with Axe. He says it smells like cigarette smoke, maybe even like pot. Undoubtedly, the creators of Axe did this on purpose; it's probably why the deodorant is so popular with teenagers. If their parents tell them they smell like smoke, they can claim that it's Axe and not get in trouble.

But at some point I am convinced that I am no longer smelling Axe, I really am smelling smoke.

I blame myself for this, of course. If my child smells like cigarettes, it can only mean that I Am a Terrible Mother.

I confront Taz about the smoke, and he denies, repeatedly and vociferously, that he has ever smoked a cigarette.

This turns me into a Crazy Woman who skulks around the house sniffing everything, like a dog. I sniff his hair, his coat, his laundry, his backpack. I check out garbage cans for cigarette butts, look in drawers for I don't know what. Then one night I'm certain—certain, for once!—that I really do smell smoke as he walks in.

I confront him again. He insists he was merely around others who were smoking.

"Like secondhand smoke won't kill you?" I scream, following him into the living room as I launch into a litany of all the relatives whose smoking led to cancer and emphysema and other disgusting diseases, none of whom could be here today to recite the dangers of smoking because THEY ARE ALL DEAD!

He turns away from me and sits down at the computer. But I'm on a roll now, and the lack of eye contact won't stop me from really getting into my rant.

"Don't you remember how my aunt up in Maine used to cough and spit out all that stuff, and how she had that oxygen tube stuck in her nose, all because she smoked cigarettes?" I continue.

He and his brother, Sport, really liked that aunt, despite the coughing and oxygen tubes, because she always bought them a big bag of barbecue potato chips any time she knew they were coming to visit. (It always amazes me how easy it is to win a kid over. You don't have to take them to Disney or buy them a Wii. You just have to be a reliable source of some really awful kind of junk food.)

I have one last image in my arsenal to make my point. "Didn't I tell you that your grandfather had emphysema when he died, and how sad it is that he didn't live long enough to get to know you and your brother . . ." But here my voice trails off; I can't rant about that. It makes me too sad.

Besides, I suddenly realize that Taz does not appear to have heard a word I've said. Instead of listening to me, he is sitting at the computer, instant-messaging forty-five of his closest friends simultaneously.

No matter. I have a great windup for my speech, and I'm not giving up just because my audience couldn't care less. "And the next time you come home smelling like cigarettes, you can take all your clothes off outside the door, in front of the neighbors, because I don't want that stink in my house!"

A friend of mine told me she knew another mother who'd gotten results with that line, so I figured I'd try it. And lo and behold, the threat of a public stripping grabs his attention.

"OK," he says, turning around for a moment to finally acknowledge my existence. "Calm down! Don't worry! I get it."

He turns back to the screen. I creep up and look over his shoulder. Now he's on his MySpace page, where no doubt he is being stalked by dozens of perverts. I remind myself silently that I Am a Terrible Mother.

In the personal profile section of his MySpace entry, he has written that he is twenty-two years old. Next to "favorite books," he has written, "I hate books." (Terrible Mother, Terrible Mother, TERRIBLE MOTHER!)

For a photo of his alleged twenty-two-year-old self, he has posted a picture taken at Six Flags, in which he is standing next to Bugs Bunny.

Music pulses softly from the computer speaker. He has figured out how to stitch some hip-hop into his MySpace page. Undoubtedly, that is in violation of the music industry's copyright laws, which means that his MySpace page is not only fraudulent because it misrepresents his age, but it is also illegal. The music starts with an ominous synthesized beat—*ba, ba, ba, BA BA BA baaah, ba ba ba, BA BA BA baaah*—and then I hear a thuglike voice chanting:

> *This is why I'm HOT*
> *This is why I'm HOT.*

Suddenly, the IMs are flying.

"WASSUP" reads a message.

"NM," he types in. "JC."

A few months back, I would have been trying to figure out why "New Mexico" and "Junior Cadets" were the appropriate responses to the question "What's up?" But by now I had done enough spying to know that "NM, JC" stands for "Nothin' much, just chillin'." (I also know OMG is "oh my God," and LOL is "laugh out loud," which makes a lot more sense as a response to jokes than when I thought it stood for "lots of love." I know WTF, too, but I'm too much of a lady to tell you what that means.)

I glance at the screen name of Taz's correspondent. It's a girl. But just as I start to feel smug about my abilities as a MySpace Mata Hari, he senses me behind him and puts his hand over the screen.

"Go away!" he shouts.

"OK," I say, and slowly back away. As I make my retreat, he starts flipping through a dozen other MySpace pages, and I recognize some of the photos. A few are kids from his middle school, and a few I actually recognize from his kindergarten class.

But the boys look so large now, and sort of scary. They have . . . ugh, dark hair growing over their lips. They wear baseball caps with logos that look to me like gang symbols. They smirk. Stare. And scowl.

The girls are even scarier, but for different reasons: They look grown-up and beautiful. They have long wavy hair and wear sexy little camisole tops, and they smile and flirt for the camera.

An image pops into my mind of a photo of some of these kids from a birthday party when Taz was little. They were small and sweet then. They wore dopey little cone paper hats with elastic chin straps. My sister had painted cat's whiskers on their faces, and we'd made necklaces out of dried rigatoni and played Pin the Tail on the Monster, a creature I'd let them draw on a big piece of brown paper taped to the wall.

In the photo I'm thinking of, Taz had his cheeks puckered, ready to blow out the candles on a cake I'd made. I remember that day felt like an important milestone. We were moving from tricycles to training wheels, from being a little boy to being just a kid. It seemed like a very big deal.

Fast forward eight years to Taz's bar mitzvah, when he turned thirteen. He was wearing a suit and tie, and everyone at the party kept walking up to him saying, "Today you are a man!" in a fake deep voice and cracking up. But Elon and I didn't think it was so funny when we saw the way those eighth-grade girls in their high-heeled shoes were hanging all over him.

Still, I could see that the thirteenth birthday was a turning point, too, just like when he'd turned five. Childhood had abruptly given way to adolescence. All the little triumphs that had seemed so important along the way suddenly felt unremarkable—learning to swim and skate, memorizing times tables, crossing the street, and walking to school without a grown-up.

Now all those accomplishments seemed like one big given, the inevitable result of a little boy growing up. But if I pushed myself, I could find, at the edges of my maternal memory, the details that proved each of those achievements was incredibly hard-won. Like his father steadying him on a two-wheeler day after day until he could pedal a few yards on his own without falling over. How many times did Elon jog around the block, following that wobbly little bike to make sure there were no accidents, kidnappings, or hit-and-runs?

And how we worried for days after Taz started walking to school alone in third grade that something terrible might happen to him. The worry intensified three grades later into sheer parental terror when he started middle school in another neighborhood and had to take the train to school. Parents in other parts of the country worry when their kindergartners first take the school bus, and when their teenagers first get learner's permits, but we live in New York, where the parental nervous breakdown comes when your kid starts riding the subway without you.

I comforted myself by noting that at least Taz wasn't *driving* the train, he was merely a passenger. But what if he got lost? What if he got mugged? What if he lost his fare card? What if a crazy person pushed him on the tracks or tried to kidnap him?

The first few days of his new commute, Elon and I went with him, morning and afternoon. I wasn't sure how we were going to keep doing this, given that we both work full-time, but I wasn't thinking that far ahead. By the third day, though, Taz had had enough of our mollycoddling.

"Just what do you think is going to happen to me?" he demanded.

Not wanting to frighten him with my paranoid visions of disaster, I said, "You might get lost."

"I'll prove to you that I won't," he said. "Follow me, and don't say a word."

It was around 9 p.m. on a Wednesday night. I didn't particularly feel like leaving the house at that hour just to test his sense of direction. But he nagged me until I relented. He was determined to go to school the next day by himself, and getting me to test him that night was the only way he could think of to get me off his back.

Wordlessly, I followed as he made the trip that night to school and back without any interference from me. When we got off the train near home, he turned to me triumphantly.

"See? I did it!"

Instantly, my brain was flooded with a hundred what-ifs. I decided to quiz him.

What if a scary person got on the train and started staring at him?

"I would stand next to a nice-looking lady and pretend that she was my mom."

I was impressed. "What if the train skipped your stop?"

"I would get off at the next stop and take the train back."

Then came the trivia. I quizzed him on transfers, train lines, directions, neighborhoods, and everything else I could think of. Quick as a winning *Jeopardy* contestant, he fired off every answer flawlessly until I was exhausted.

"OK, then, now can I go to school by myself?"

What could I say? I had to give in. I made him promise to call me on his cell phone before he got on the train and when he got off the train. Though exactly how this would help him if someone was trying to kill him wasn't clear to either of us. Still, it made me feel better.

Little did I know that the cell phone I was counting on to rescue him would soon become the monster that ate my bank account. He goes over his minutes every month, by a lot, and it's not from calling me. They have to mail the bill in a ten-by-fourteen envelope, it's so big.

I make him pay back every cent over the basic charge, but that doesn't seem to stop him from exceeding the limit every time. I could just not pay the bill, but it's not like it used to be, where they cut off service if you owe. Now they wreck your credit rating, too. I could take the phone away, but then when it's 8 p.m. and I don't know where he is, how am I going to find him?

Sure, he's getting too big to kidnap, but what about the crazies who might push him onto a subway track? What about drivers who don't yield to pedestrians? What about muggers looking to steal a wallet or an iPod or the very cell phone I'd hoped would keep him safe?

One night, as he heads out the door to get pizza with

some friends, I remind him about kids we know who were mugged—one outside school, one on a bus, one at knifepoint near our house.

"Mom," he says, "I'm not stupid!"

"I know you're not stupid," I say. "Just be careful."

"Mom," he says, "I'm un-JUMP-able."

That's a new word for me. But as he pulls up the hood of his oversized sweatshirt (reminding me of another word, *hoodlum*), I suddenly see him and his friends the way someone else would. They are hulking. Rowdy. Horsing around. Cursing, high-fiving, laughing about some private joke. If I was walking toward them, I would probably cross the street.

They really do look . . . unjumpable.

"See you later, Mom. I love you!"

What?

He said, "I love you," to his mother in front of his friends? I'm stunned.

As they file out, one kid knocks the dog's water dish over, another steps on the cat's tail. They're pushing and shouting and singing snatches of a rap song, one of them chanting, "I love it when you call me . . ." and all the others chiming in, "Big POP-pa!"

Finally, the door slams.

Then it opens again.

"Mom," he says, "can you give me ten dollars?"

Sighing, I reach for my wallet. "Get juice, not soda! No candy! No pepperoni! It's not good for you, all that sugar, all that fat. I don't want you to get diabetes!

There's an obesity epidemic in this country, do you know that?"

I interrupt myself to hand him a $20 bill. "I want change from that, OK?" I say.

"Thanks." He smiles.

We both know that twenty dollars is as good as spent.

# ARE WE THERE YET?

*T*here we were on the mini golf course, where we've been going for years for a fun day with the kids while on vacation up in Maine.

As we walked in from the parking lot, I smiled at the comforting sight of the kitschy little turning windmill that you hit the balls through, and the hole that looks like a tiny cemetery with fake tombstones. And I was really looking forward to a scoop of ice cream after the game from the nearby stand selling Gifford's, a creamy local brand with a zillion interesting flavors. Flavors like pumpkin and maple and peppermint with little crunchy pieces of candy inside.

This, I thought to myself contentedly, was what a good-old-fashioned family vacation was all about. Togetherness. Quality time! An afternoon where your biggest worry is whether you're going to go for the pistachio or the butter pecan.

Suddenly, my reverie was interrupted by the sound

of raised voices. Familiar raised voices. I realized that Elon and Taz were having a huge fight.

"You're going to play mini golf with us whether you like it or not!" I heard my husband growl, to which Taz wailed something about hating his family more than anything in the world.

Welcome to the family vacation, starring an angst-ridden, friend-deprived thirteen-year-old, who experiences humiliation every second of every day simply because his parents exist. Apparently, that feeling had reached a climactic intensity on the mini golf course.

The specific issue here, other than the generally embarrassing context of an adolescent having to appear in public with his parents and little brother, was that the kid realized his cell phone could get service at the mini golf course. He wanted to call his friends instead of playing with his family.

My sister and I vacation in a little cottage on a pond in Maine, about fifteen miles from this mini golf course, which is located in the town of Skowhegan. There is no cell service in our house on the pond. (Not only that, no cable TV, video games, or Internet service, either. Just a well-worn Monopoly game and a canoe. Could I have ordered up any greater torture for an adolescent?)

But on the golf course in town, not only was there a strong cell signal, it was even free—no roaming charges! From Taz's point of view, why shouldn't he use this opportunity to call all the thirteen-year-olds he hadn't spoken to in two weeks and say profound and cool teenage things? Like, "So, whassup?"

I had never realized before how much my son has in common with African wildebeests, but it suddenly hit me that deprived of his herd, this young mammal was becoming disoriented. He needed, with an almost physical urgency, to be roaming the savanna with the other animals. Forced to spend twenty-four hours a day with his parents and little brother, he was starting to lose his identity.

His separation from friends while on vacation not only included lack of phone contact, but because he couldn't go online on the computer, he also had no access to instant messaging. MySpace had become NoSpace. Facebook was Faceless. The deprivation had actually led him to beg to go to the town library a few times—not to get books, mind you, but in order to attempt to make contact with his friends, using the library computer.

Back on the mini golf course, I tried to make peace between father and son.

"Please," I pleaded, "please stop fighting! Please don't raise your voices! It's only mini golf!"

All around us, happy families putted away—in between taking sneak peeks at our dysfunctional unit in full pitched battle before we even played the first hole.

"What's the problem?" I whispered. "Can't we just work something out here?"

"I'm really homesick!" whined Taz, his face creased in pain. "I miss my friends! I just want to talk to some of them, and I finally got a cell signal here! Why do I have to play mini golf?"

Elon turned to me, fuming. "Why can't he just be a part of this family? We came here to play mini golf and he's ruining a perfectly nice day!"

Eventually, I brokered a compromise worthy of the Nobel Peace Prize. Taz would play mini golf, but he would play one hole behind the rest of us, while talking to his friends back home on his cell phone. I hovered between him and the rest of the family, making sure to write down everyone's score and enforce the truce.

The cell phone was cradled between his shoulder and his ear as he swung the club on the second hole, hitting a hole in one.

A giant grin spread across his face. He held the phone away from his face. "Mom, did you see that?" he said excitedly.

I nodded and felt a little twinge flashbacking to when he was about eight years old and was finally coordinated enough to get the ball in the little hole.

Then he shoved the phone back between his shoulder and his ear. "Yo," he said to his friend on the other end of the line, "I'm up in Maine, playing mini golf. And it's mad fun."

I was just glad he wasn't telling his friend about the other horrible thing his mother did to him on vacation.

The night before we left home, I had accidentally erased all the songs off his iPod, so he was also deprived of his music.

I swear, I didn't mean to do it! And to his credit, he was very good-natured about the incident, I guess because it confirmed his smug view of me as a complete technological ninny. Which I totally admit that I am.

But really, how was I supposed to know that if the iPod is plugged into the computer and you turn the computer off, the iPod is wiped clean? I was only trying to cut down on the electric bill by shutting everything off before we left for vacation. (This might be a good time to also admit that I later washed the same iPod in the laundry by accident, and when I fessed up, Taz didn't get mad about that, either.) Looking back, though, I can honestly say that this business of my thirteen-year-old being too important to spend time with his family on vacation actually started with a road trip we took when Taz was twelve. At home, see, I was too busy doing the laundry and making dinner to notice that my kid had started to despise me. But on vacation, when we actually had to be together twenty-four hours a day, well, there was no denying then that Taz's idea of a good time didn't necessarily involve us.

The road trip took place about three months before Taz's thirteenth birthday. At the time, I perceived some of the incidents on that trip as isolated, amusing little quirks. But I see now that they actually constituted a turning point—or maybe even a morphing point—

where taking your kids on a wonderful family trip becomes less like a Disney commercial and more like *National Lampoon's Vacation* or *Little Miss Sunshine* (a movie I loved because it made me realize that some families are even more dysfunctional than mine).

To put these incidents in context and fully appreciate them, you need to know a little bit more about us. I make my living as a travel editor, so you'd think that planning a family trip would be easy. But actually my job does not require me to go anywhere; I just sit at a desk in New York and read about fabulous places that other people get to go to. Oh, and I also correct their grammar. (Please don't get me started on *its* and *it's*.)

The trip planner in the family is actually Elon, who, I think it is fair to say, is slightly obsessive about this sort of thing. This particular road trip, for example, was eighteen days long. And if, for some reason, I needed to know six months in advance where we were going to be on the afternoon of the eleventh day, he could pretty much tell me exactly, because he'd planned the whole trip out in three-hour blocks. Before it was over, we'd driven three thousand miles through six western states, plus the Grand Canyon, Yosemite, and ten more national parks (but who's counting?). P.S. Did I mention Universal, Vegas, and Disney?

We started our trip in San Francisco, staying with my cousin Stuart. Stuart is a real-life private detective, and as we went around town with him, he kept pointing out homicide scenes he'd investigated. As New Yorkers, this made us feel right at home.

Stuart also lives around the corner from Haight-Ashbury. "Oh my God, that's so cool," I said when I saw the street signs at the intersection.

"What? Why is it cool?" asked Taz, but I refused to tell him.

A few days later, I got a glimpse, almost without realizing it, of what life with a teenager was going to be like. Taz's reaction to our visit to Sequoia National Park was definitely what my tenth-grade English teacher referred to in *Tess of the D'Urbervilles* as an ironic foreshadowing.

We had driven to Sequoia to see the largest trees on earth—the General Grant Tree, the General Sherman Tree, and all the rest. But Taz immediately pronounced them the "Generally Boring Trees." We set out to hike the loop trail to see more of these amazing phenomena, but after about a quarter mile, Taz just couldn't take it. He started hyperventilating and bent over, clutching his stomach.

"Is it the bacon burrito you had for lunch?" I said, genuinely alarmed.

"No, I just can't stand it here! These trees—they're so stupid! I gotta get back to the car!"

"You must be kidding me!" I said. "Would you mind explaining to me what exactly is so bad about being in the woods with your family in the presence of these incredible trees? You don't like the color green? You're mad because there are no electric outlets to plug your phone charger into?"

But before I even finished asking the question, Taz took off and started running back to the parking lot.

Elon and I looked at each other in disbelief. Here we were, walking through one of the country's most amazing national parks, on an absolutely beautiful day, in the shadows of these ancient, majestic trees, so big around that six people holding hands and stretching their arms out couldn't begin to make a circle around them. And our son couldn't care less! What a wretch of a boy! What was wrong with him?

Then Elon started freaking out.

"What if he gets lost?" he said.

"It's a loop trail," I said. "He'll be fine."

"What if something happens to him? What if someone KIDNAPS him?"

"What, you think he's going to be kidnapped by a big tree?"

But you know how it is when you're a parent. Once you utter the *K* word, once you've allowed that thought to enter your mind, there is no going back to being calm. You've crossed the parental bridge that leads from rationality to mental breakdown. Your thoughts are now flooded with every horrible kidnapping story you ever heard of, and the only cure is to physically get hold of your child—before, of course, someone else does.

Since Taz was now out of sight, that meant Elon would have to run ahead to catch him and protect him from the Forces of Evil lurking behind the General Grant Tree in Sequoia National Park. Elon took off, and I was left with Sport, who seemed to take it all in stride. Within moments, Elon had disappeared down the trail, so Sport and I just held hands and trudged along the path to reunite with them.

Sport was just seven years old at the time, really just as sweet as could be and still young enough to be filled with wonder when I pointed out a pine cone the size of a Chihuahua. As it turned out, though, we were rewarded with an even more remarkable sight. A mama bear and her cub were cavorting in a glade, just above the trail.

"Oh, Mommy, let's run and tell Taz and Dad!" he said.

I should have been touched by Sport's sweet impulse, to not want his brother and father to miss out on such a special thing. But at the moment I couldn't focus on that. I was too busy freaking out. It wasn't kidnappers we had to worry about on this trail. It was wild animals! I knew even more stories about bears attacking people, especially children, who are small and delicious, than I did about kidnappers.

I grabbed him and moved back from the edge of the path. "Don't run away from me," I said quietly. "Don't go any nearer to the bears than we already are. They might try to eat you."

To his credit, he didn't get upset. After all, a kid who grows up in New York City is raised with all kinds of crazy warnings. Was the concept of a bear wanting to eat him scarier than the thought of a crazy person pushing him in front of an oncoming train? Not really. So we crouched low across the way, took a few not-very-good pictures, and let the noisy German tourists who were walking behind us scare the bears back into the woods. After a few moments, I even relaxed a little and started to appreciate how special it was that we had gotten to see this. (Not to mention how miraculous it was that we hadn't been mauled to death.)

"Taz is going to be sad that he missed them," Sport said when we resumed our hike.

But actually, Taz was just as happy to be back in the car, where he had convinced Elon to turn on the air-conditioning and the radio. We told him that he'd missed the bears, and he told us that we'd missed hearing Gwen Stefani on this great station he'd found.

The next day we hit L.A. Before the trip, I'd told each child they could pick one thing that would be their special adventure. Sport picked Disneyland, naturally. But Taz surprised me with the sophisticated nature of his request.

"I want to have brunch at The Ivy," he said.

I wasn't even sure what The Ivy was. I mean, it sounded vaguely familiar, but why, I didn't know. Then Taz's weekly issue of *Us* magazine arrived. I leafed through it, as I always do, hoping to feel superior when the Fashion Police picked on an outfit that I, too, found hideous on Mary-Kate Olsen. I also enjoyed testing my own judgment against the "Who wore it better?" survey where two celeb chicks wearing the same designer gown are judged by a hundred people surveyed on the street. (It was always so reassuring to see that the girl with the most cleavage didn't always win the day.)

Then a photo of Julia Roberts caught my eye. The caption said she was eating lunch at The Ivy with her agent! In the following weeks, I noticed that every single issue included a picture of someone famous eating at The Ivy. How did my not-quite-thirteen-year-old son from Brooklyn end up with a yen for a restaurant frequented by Hollywood power brokers? The photos in *Us* were the missing link.

But I am a Big Nobody. How was I going to get a reservation there? How would I ever persuade Elon that we could afford to eat at a place where Julia Roberts was a regular?

Well, it turned out it wasn't that hard. Seriously, I've had more trouble ordering pizza deliveries back home than I did getting a table at The Ivy. I just called the place up and reserved a table for four, no problem. ( I considered using a phony name like Mrs. T. Cruise, but didn't.)

In the end, we didn't see any celebrities there, just a lot of other tourists like us, taking photos of their pancakes and looking around just in case a famous person happened to skateboard by. (None did.)

But they did treat us so well that we felt like celebrities, and we were even joined at our table by a producer. Well, truth be told, it was only my cousin Ben, who's worked on a couple of movies and, like a lotta folks out there, has some deals in the works. Still, it was cool to be at a table with someone making cell phone calls to confirm the pitch meeting scheduled for the next day.

And although it was the most expensive brunch I've ever had, it still came to under $200 for the five of us. A small price to pay to achieve nirvana for a twelve-year-old. His heavenly mode continued after The Ivy as we spent the rest of the day with Ben, hanging out at The Grove with beautiful people in sunglasses sipping lattes and window-shopping on Melrose. It felt like some glamorous photo shoot because everyone was so trendy looking, except for us—four schlubby people from Brooklyn, including one adolescent with a beatific look on his face.

Disney was supposed to be our last stop in California, but Elon decided to make a hundred-mile detour to spend thirty minutes at Joshua Tree National Park. Was it worth it? I'll let you guess. We made a similar detour at Elon's behest to see the giant meteor crater in Arizona and the Petrified Forest, which Elon had visited as a child on a road trip with his parents. Isn't it sad how we have to revisit our childhood traumas in order to heal them? Taz thought the Petrified Forest was even less exciting than Sequoia. There weren't even any bears.

But as we took our daily four-hour drive to wherever, I realized I was getting used to the Road Trip Life. It was actually kinda fun. We played Geography, took pictures out the window, and I started to relax about the children's insistence on eating cheddar cheese potato chips for breakfast.

I gave myself foot massages with lotion purloined from hotel bathrooms, and I sang softly to myself, lyrics from the seventies that had popped into my head after an absence of thirty years. "Been to the desert on a horse with no name," I intoned, followed by, "Standin' on a corner in Winslow, Arizona."

One of the biggest changes from the time your kids are little to the time they become adolescents is that they can't bear to hear you sing. I don't have a bad voice—I really don't. And when Taz was little, I sang all the time. I had entire books of children's songs and folk songs that we used to spend hours looking through, singing all the songs. I played them on guitar and on the piano. I taught him to sing harmony to Cat Stevens's "Wild World," and he knew all the words to "Joe Hill" by the time he was five.

But there is nothing more horrifying to a proto-teenager than to have to hear his mother sing. It must be some hormonal aversion, perhaps because it is a reminder that once he was a tiny little boy in diapers, sitting on my knee, looking at me with big eyes, thinking I was the most marvelous, magical being in all the universe because I could sing twenty-five verses of "Old MacDonald," with ever-more wondrous animals in every stanza.

Perhaps my effort to channel Don Henley in the car as we drove down Route 66 past the very Winslow, Arizona, corner mentioned in "Take It Easy" was too strong a reminder to my son that the woman whose voice now repelled him like nails on a blackboard not so long ago was lulling him to sleep. Whatever it was, he couldn't stand it.

"SHUT UP!" he screamed as I got to the part about "a flatbed Ford, slowin' down to take a look at me."

"What? What is it? What's the matter?"

"Stop singing," he said. "I don't want to hear you singing!"

I suppose I should have been insulted, but his tone of voice was—although he is male—positively premenstrual. It was pretty clear that this was not about me, or the song, or my voice. It was about him, and his mood, and his age.

Fortunately, I had bought a small cardboard box of wine at the last 7-Eleven we stopped at. I took it out of the bag, stuck a straw in it, and started sipping. So what if I hadn't had lunch yet? I was on vacation. Time to live a little.

Besides, I needed to fortify myself for the day ahead. Our next stop was the Grand Canyon.

We arrived in late afternoon and jostled with hundreds of Japanese tourists for the best view. But guess what? The view is, um, pretty much the same no matter where you stand. The kids were underwhelmed.

"It's just a big hole in the ground," Taz complained.

"What?" I said. "You total ingrate! Your father planned this trip for months and we drove thousands of miles across the desert to get here! The least you could do is pretend to be impressed."

"I just didn't think it would be so boring."

"Well, don't tell your father. He might throw himself over the edge."

But Elon was in his own little world by then. In his glory, in fact. Breathing in the deep, clear canyon air. Grinning from ear to ear as he strode around the rim, pointing out the variegated rock and the little ribbon of river at the bottom.

"Isn't it great to be on vacation with our family, seeing things like this?" he said to no one in particular. "Why, I remember visiting the Grand Canyon with my parents when I was a boy! And it's just as glorious now as it was then!"

"When's dinner?" asked Taz. "I'm hungry."

We had a good meal at one of the park lodges, then turned in early. Elon was planning to wake us for a sunrise hike.

"Won't it be great to see that sun come up over the canyon?" he said just before we fell asleep. "I bet it will be beautiful!"

We were all still sleeping when the alarm went off, piercing the darkness of the night.

It was 5 a.m. but it felt like 2.

"Rise and shine, everybody!" Elon called out with glee. "Time for our sunrise hike!"

I dragged myself out of bed, struggled into my clothes, and attempted to wake my children.

"Why are you waking me up when it's still dark outside?" Taz whined. "I'm trying to sleep!"

At least he eventually got up. Sport simply could not be roused. I finally pulled his pants on him while he was still sleeping and tied his shoes for him, then slung him over my shoulder and carried him out of the hotel. The jostling woke him. It was starting to get a little bit light. At least I didn't have to feel bad that I hadn't brought a miner's headlamp to light my way.

"Are we going home?" Sport asked dreamily.

"No," I said. "We're just going to relive another of Daddy's childhood traumas."

Sport nodded sweetly and shook himself awake, then gamely climbed down out of my arms to walk on his own. Elon led the way, with me and Sport in the middle, then Taz dragging slowly behind.

"Hurry up," Elon kept shouting back, the word *up* softly echoing off the canyon walls. "We don't want to miss the sunrise!"

We started climbing down the Bright Angel Trail. It kept getting lighter and lighter out, but, strangely, no matter which direction we looked, the promised sunrise never materialized. There weren't any colored clouds low in the sky, either. Finally, after we'd been walking for forty-five minutes, we realized the day had dawned without our witnessing the promised celestial phenomenon.

Then it hit me.

"Elon," I said. "I don't know how to break this to you, but you can't see the sunrise from inside the Grand Canyon."

He looked at me and I could see the logic building in his brain.

The sunrise can only be seen on the horizon.

There is no horizon when you've hiked down the trail into the canyon.

By the time the sun is high enough in the sky to be seen over the top of the canyon walls, it's well into the morning.

There might have been a beautiful sunrise that day, but we would have had to be somewhere else to see it.

"Oh," he said sadly. "I guess you're right."

"Isn't there going to be a sunrise?" asked Sport. "When are we going to see it?"

Taz actually thought this was pretty funny. He started snickering.

"There is no sunrise!" he said to his brother gleefully. "Mom and Dad are so stupid, they thought we could see the sunrise from inside the Grand Canyon, but that's impossible!"

Just then a caravan of donkeys carrying riders crossed our path. We flattened ourselves against the side of the canyon to let them by. The tourists riding them were smiling. They looked happy and rested. They'd gotten a lot more sleep than we did, and they didn't have to walk down like we did.

And now the worst part: We had to walk back up, making sure all the while that we didn't step in the steaming piles of donkey poop along the trail. We finally made it back, went and got some breakfast, and packed up our hotel room. The kids were so tired they could barely keep their heads up. I forced them to pose on a little bench with the canyon in the background, but the looks on their faces in that photo said it all: "I'm exhausted, and I hate you."

They then collapsed in the car. On the way out of the park, as we followed the road around the canyon rim, Elon kept pulling over at one scenic lookout after another.

"Come on, guys! Get out and take a look! It's spectacular!" he enthused at every stop. To tell the truth, I was kind of excited. I liked taking pictures of all the different views. But the children refused to leave the van.

"I'm not getting up until we reach the next hotel," Taz said.

Eventually, after a number of hours, or days, I can't remember which (and besides, time was starting to flow into some endless psychedelic continuum out there in the desert), we ended up in Utah.

Bryce Canyon, Utah, to be precise, which is known for having one of the darkest night skies in the Lower Forty-eight. We were going to go stargazing in the park that night, as soon as it got dark. I got some take-out food from the restaurant at the hotel and brought it back to the room, and we chowed down. The sun would soon be gone, and then we'd head out for a look at the heavens.

I was really looking forward to this. What a great family outing, especially for two city boys like mine, to get to see the stars in all their awe-inspiring glory. I was sure it would be a wonderful memory for all of us.

"I'm not going."

Who said that? Did I hear right?

It was Taz.

We'd driven twenty-five hundred miles to this god-forsaken place to see the freaking Big Dipper and God knows what else up there in the goddamn night sky and he has the nerve to tell us that he's not going stargazing?

"What?" Elon said. He had that crazed look on his face, the same one he gets when Taz's cell phone bill arrives, a cross between incredulity, as in "I cannot believe this is happening!" and fury, as in "I'm going to kill someone!"

"I'm not going," Taz said flatly. "I don't want to go stargazing."

"Why?" I said. Or maybe even screamed.

"I already know what the stars look like. I saw them last summer up in Maine."

Well, that was true. On our little pond up in Maine, there are no nearby lights, and the night sky is pretty darn dark. In fact, sometimes it's so dark out there that I get totally spooked and run around locking all the doors and windows, checking the phone for a dial tone. (Hey, there's a reason Stephen King sets all his stories in Maine, and I don't want to be the inspiration for his next book.)

"But it's not like there's anything else to do here," I said, trying to be reasonable. "You might as well just get in the car and come with us. What are you going to do here by yourself?"

"I'm watching the MTV Video Music Awards," he said calmly and with determination, reaching for the remote. "I already called the front desk and I know what station they're on, and they start at eight p.m., right when you're going to the park. I don't want to miss them. They're in Miami, and P. Diddy's hosting."

As he spoke, he picked up the remote, found the channel, and put the show on. The preshow had started, with footage of all the stars arriving by yacht or limo, depending on their preference.

"Taz isn't coming with us?" asked Sport sadly.

"He can't just stay here!" Elon said to me angrily. "You let him get away with murder!"

"You can say no," I said. "I didn't say it was OK."

"Yeah, but you didn't say it *wasn't* OK."

"Oh sure, blame me!" I said.

"Well, why do I always have to be the bad guy? Why can't you say no sometimes?"

I considered this for a moment, but quickly realized why.

"Truthfully," I said, "I just don't care that much. It's stargazing in Utah. It's not the SATs."

Besides, after the early morning hike at the Grand Canyon didn't exactly work out, I was starting to wonder if maybe Taz had a sixth sense about whether these things were all they were cracked up to be.

Elon sighed. His posture was one of Defeated Dad.

He walked out to the car, muttering under his breath about how our family was falling apart.

Sport by now was starting to get interested in the MTV Awards; Jamie Foxx was arriving, and we'd all seen *Ray* together. Elon would be devastated if we lost Sport to the show, too, so I grabbed him by the shoulder, then pushed him out the door. I took one longing look back at the screen, where some beauty I'd never heard of was describing her glittering, skintight gown for the camera after she stepped out of her coach.

"Are you coming?" I heard Elon shouting from the parking spot outside our room.

"Coming!" I said.

The park was just a few minutes' drive from the hotel. It was, indeed, pitch black out. We were in the middle of nowhere. I started wondering if Utah had a horror writer along the lines of Maine's. We almost missed the turnoff for the park, but the sign suddenly appeared in our headlights. Elon pulled in to a parking area where we could see the sky framed between several tall ponderosa pines, their beautiful shaggy branches framed black against the dark blue sky.

It was indeed a glorious sight, thousands of stars swirling in front of us. The Big Dipper was easy to find, and we could pick out the shapes of other constellations, too, though we weren't sure what any of them were called.

"I feel like I could pick the stars right out of the sky," Sport whispered to me.

I hugged him. It was so nice to still have one little boy in the family.

We didn't stay too long. And when we got back, the MTV Awards show was still going strong.

We all stayed up late watching it.

Even Elon.

## *YOUR BOXERS ARE SHOWING*

*I* have learned many things from my thirteen-year-old. One of them is that style goes right down to your underwear.

If you pose the boxers-or-briefs question in my house, my husband will definitely say briefs. Elon is a tighty-whities Fruit of the Loom type of guy. Always has been, always will be.

But even though I weaned Taz from diapers to briefs, somewhere along the line he gravitated to boxers. And not just any boxers, but boxers in the wildest patterns imaginable. Colorful paisleys, dice and dominos, quotes from movies, green hundred-dollar bills, red-and-white hearts, even a picture of Al Pacino in *Scarface*. ("Say hello to my leetle friend!" Great slogan for underwear, huh?) Once I bought him some plain blue boxers—what was I thinking?—but he never wore them. A friend is preserving her adolescent son's array of patterned boxers by making a quilt for him out of the ones he has outgrown.

She envisions him taking the quilt to college, and I can totally see this becoming a trend.

"Nice quilt!" some girl living down the hall of the dorm will say. "Was it made from the fabric of, like, family heirlooms?"

"Nah. My mom sewed it using old boxers from when I was thirteen."

Some fashions, of course, I can see with my own two eyes, like when all of a sudden everyone has the same hairdo or the same boots. But under normal circumstances, you wouldn't think it would be so easy to tell whether your kid's underwear is in style. After all, you don't usually see what type of underpants the average person is wearing, and unless someone is running for president, you don't normally walk up and ask whether they prefer boxers or briefs.

But in this case, it has become obvious to me that, as usual, my son has chosen the impeccably trendy path. Many young guys now wear their pants so low on their hips that the tops of their boxers are visible, so I can see for myself that this is indeed the style. It's become so pervasive, in fact, that a couple of towns around the country have deemed it a form of public lewdness and sought to make it illegal.

Even if I couldn't actually see that half the guys on the street are wearing boxers, when I go shopping with Taz, it is impossible to ignore the fact that there are entire departments devoted to boxers.

Briefs, in contrast, are usually displayed in sterile little plastic envelopes hanging on hooks on one compact solitary shelf. After all, there isn't much to choose from other than size; they all look alike, and they're usually white.

But the boxers are displayed in rooms the size of football stadiums. They hang on racks, like designer dresses, and they are usually being studied and worshipped by crowds of men. I feel a little uncomfortable standing around there with Taz, to tell you the truth, and I get a few weird looks—the kind of looks that women always give the lone guy picking his nose in the bra department. But I don't care—I'm just not ready to let my son pick out his own underwear. I swear, it's not that I'm a control freak. But if I left it up to him, he'd buy the $45 Dolce & Gabbana boxers instead of the $10 Hanes, so I gotta stick it out despite the funny looks.

Now, while I draw the line at expensive underwear, I have caved in to some extent on absurdly expensive footwear. For years, I bought shoes for Taz and Sport at discount stores like Payless where you could get one pair for $19.99 and a second pair for another five or ten bucks. So what if the shoes fell apart after a few months? Kids' feet grow so fast, by the time the shoes had holes in them, they'd be too small, anyway.

But with the start of middle school came resistance to the cheapo sneakers of childhood. Taz wanted shoes in bright colors with thick soles and shiny uppers, named for athletes, and bought in specialty stores. When he was ten and eleven, his feet were still small enough that he could find a style to suit his taste for under $50. And I could see that most of these shoes were in fact better made than the $20 varieties. So I gave in to the price tag and rationalized it on the grounds that at least they lasted a little longer than the discount brands.

But by the time he turned twelve, he was wearing men's sizes, and the types of shoes he wanted were now running a hundred bucks and up. Despite what you may have read about women being obsessed with shoes, not all of us care to spend our hard-earned money on fancy footwear. I personally have never spent a hundred dollars on shoes, and I don't think I ever will. Under $50 is my usual price range for my shoes, though I will go higher for boots or leather that looks like it will last a few years.

So why, given my own budget for shoes, would I pay more than that for kids' shoes? Well, Taz had all kinds of bogus reasons, but the one I liked best of all was when he told me it was a safety issue. If he didn't have cool shoes, he argued, the other kids would tease him. Maybe even beat him up.

This was completely contrary to everything I'd read about expensive kids' shoes becoming targets of theft. (Besides, aren't my tax dollars supposed to be hard at work making all the schools "bully-free"?) I had been under the impression that if you had expensive shoes, someone might shoot you just to get them. But Taz assured me that the risk of being smacked around for being uncool was way higher than the risk of being robbed of your Jordans.

When I thought about it, I realized that this argument resonated with me to some extent. When I was a teenager, the most humiliating thing that could happen to you was having pants that were too short. I'm five-foot-nine and I grew a lot in junior high, so my pants were never long enough because I was constantly outgrowing them, and constantly getting teased about them.

"Highwater, highwater, where's the flood?" was the taunt in fifth and sixth grades. In seventh and eighth, the other kids were too cool to actually say anything to put me down, but all it took was a two-second glance at my ankles—which, if I were dressed properly, should not have been visible—followed by a one-second glance at my face to make it clear that I was utterly pathetic.

In fact, I was so pathetic that the really Cool Girls wouldn't even waste their breath teasing me. They saved their spoken critiques for their friends, who were potentially salvageable, but I was just too far gone.

At the time, of course, I swore to myself that when I grew up and had kids, I would remember how awful it was to feel like a social reject because of your clothes and I would make sure my kids dressed OK.

Now that I am a mother, though, other considerations come into play. For example, I worry that reasonable people will think I'm a bad parent for giving in to the materialism that is the curse of my son's generation. And I realized one day that part of the problem here is that Taz and I want to impress people in precisely opposite ways.

I want people to think that I'm frugal, and sensible, that my kid doesn't run the show, and that I've brought him up with good values. He wants people to think that he's stylish and doesn't worry about petty things like price tags, and that he can pretty much get his parents to do anything he wants.

Finally, I forged a compromise that allowed me to feel like I had been true to my sensibilities, while allowing him to avoid the alleged gang of kids who were just waiting to beat up people wearing stupid shoes. I set a limit on how much money I was willing to spend—$50—and I agreed to fork over that amount and allow him to put it toward whatever ridiculous sum he wanted to spend on shoes as long as he made up the balance. To his credit, he saved up fifty to add to my fifty. Together, we went to look for the shoes of his dreams.

Incredibly, though, a hundred dollars wasn't even enough to buy most of the types of shoes he was looking at. The going rate seemed to be $120. As we walked in and out of the stores on the avenue where we were shopping, I started sputtering and muttering to myself. What kind of insanity was this? Most of the other shoppers appeared to be families of modest means. They weren't riding around in fancy cars! And they weren't dressed particularly well, either—except for the shoes they were looking to buy for their kids.

"This is crazy," I kept saying to Taz. "I've never spent

this kind of money on shoes. I just can't believe how much people are willing to pay." By the fourth or fifth store, our shopping expedition felt depressing. We'd never find a pair that Taz deemed fashionable enough in the price range I had set.

Finally, I couldn't take it anymore. I told Taz he needed to lower his expectations, and I headed home. He decided to keep looking on his own.

An hour later he came back wearing a pair of $120 shoes. They were Jordans, of course, and I had to admit there was something about them that was truly aesthetically appealing. They had that little logo of the jumping basketball player on the heel, and they were white quilted leather with black suede trim and black laces, with a few red details at the edges. High-tops, of course, with a hard plastic silvery inset in the arch.

But how could he afford them when he only had a hundred dollars?

He said that without me to bog him down, he was free to bargain with the manager of one of the stores we'd passed by. The guy had given him $20 off the list price. Apparently, when the salesmen see a kid with his mother, they figure the kid can talk the parent into paying what they're asking. But when a kid is by himself, they're more willing to negotiate a deal. They know that without a parent's credit card, the kid can't spend any more than the cash in his pocket.

I felt a twinge of pride at Taz's savvy. I've never negotiated a price break on anything, not in my entire life.

Not in Mexico in an outdoor market, not at a yard sale, not on used cars or real estate, and certainly not in a retail store.

I later learned that Taz had deals running with every store in the neighborhood. This one never charged him tax, this one routinely gave him a 10 percent discount, this one gave him stuff on credit. Most of these places were stores I shopped in all the time without ever establishing a relationship.

How did he do it? And what was wrong with me that I couldn't do it? The barber knew his style of haircut; I'd been going to the same hairdresser for twenty years, and each time I went in, the guy looked at me like I'd never been there before. (I'd say, "How's your godson Josh?"and he'd do a double take, as if I'd been stalking him.)

The music store guy knew Taz's taste in CDs, and the video store guy saved DVDs for him under the counter, ahead of the release date. (It sounds like ancient history to talk about CDs and video stores, but I swear it was only 2005.) One day when I went in the video store and presented our membership card to take out a movie, the attendant looked at me admiringly.

"Oh, you're Taz's mom?" he said, nodding knowingly. "He's cool."

He's cool? MY son is cool? A GROWN-UP thinks my son is cool? I was a lot of things when I was an adolescent, but I was not cool. But if my son is cool, does that make me just a little bit cool? There was something vicariously thrilling about being the mother of a Cool Boy.

And amid all the neurotic maternal anxieties I harbored about the path his life would take over the next ten years—that he wouldn't get good enough grades, that he didn't take school seriously enough, that he might not get into a good college, that he might not get a good job, that he'd end up living back home at the age of twenty-three with me doing his laundry—I comforted myself with the thought that at least I'd never have to worry that he was a dweeb.

But all of this left me feeling a little useless. As parents, our jobs include feeding, clothing, and housing our children until they are old enough to earn money to pay for these things themselves. You assume you are the middleman between your child's needs as a consumer and the marketplace's need to sell. But what good am I, when not only am I unnecessary as the intermediary, but, in the case of the sneakers, my very physical presence prevents my child from getting the object he desires?

Not only is Taz better off shopping without me because he knows what's cool and I don't, but my being there with him in the store increases the price to the point where he can't afford it. And I'm only marginally useful as a means for paying the bills, because I'm not willing to ante up what Taz thinks is a reasonable amount of money for what he wants.

On the other hand, I have to admit that those expensive sneakers really are better made than the $20 ones I used to buy. It doesn't hurt that Taz takes good care of them, wiping the dirt off and rubbing them tenderly with sneaker cleaners and leather conditioners, spraying them with waterproofing, and even storing them in their original box. I should point out here that he is far more interested in cleaning his sneakers than he is in say, cleaning his room, or even brushing his teeth.

It was different when Taz was little—and far less expensive. From pretty much the time he was born through much of elementary school, I dressed Taz in hand-me-downs. Eventually, he started to notice that an awful lot of his clothes had other people's names written in laundry marker on the labels. I can honestly say it must have been second or third grade before I took the poor kid clothes shopping, we had so many castoffs from friends and relatives in the closet.

Finally, Taz realized there was a whole world of apparel that was brand-new (not used), brightly colored (not faded), sized to fit (not whatever his cousins or neighbors had outgrown), and in style right now (not three years ago). From that point on, he pretty much refused to wear secondhand clothes. It was too thrilling to be able to go to a store and pick out exactly what he wanted.

But exactly what he wanted always seemed totally bizarre to me. Boxers and big sneakers were only part of the Look. He also liked shirts that were eight or nine sizes too big, gold chains, and, of course, pants so baggy they were falling off his butt (the better to show off his boxers).

The sneakers, by the way, were best left untied, to make it look like you just got out of prison, where they take your laces away so you won't hang yourself. My husband is a Legal Aid lawyer—who often represents inmates at Rikers Island, the city jail, and it's a little disturbing to consider how well our son fits in with his father's clients.

In addition to the overall gangsta rap look, there have also been occasional one-outfit wonders. Take the red-and-black velour track suit.

"What are you, a soccer mom?" I said incredulously when he picked out the jacket and matching pants with elasticized waistband.

But he was resolute: "That's the style, Mom!"

One of my neighbors laughed. "He looks like a Pilates instructor!" she said.

Damned if P. Diddy wasn't wearing the exact thing next time I saw him on TV. Within a few days, every kid we knew either had the same outfit or wished he had the same outfit.

Then Taz picked out an oversized white T-shirt with a picture of Wile E. Coyote on it, decorated with silver sparkles.

"Won't some big dude make fun of you for wearing that and squash your head like a cantaloupe?" I said. "It looks like the kind of thing a little girl wears to a birthday party."

"Don't worry about it," he said nonchalantly, making

it clear that my opinion was irrelevant rather than insulting. "It's hot."

The next day I was heading into work on the train and I saw two big muscled, tattooed, and otherwise scary-looking guys sitting across from me, taking up three or four seats apiece. Although the train was crowded and standing-room only, no one dared say, "Excuse me, would you mind moving over so other people could sit down?" I realized both of these guys, who looked like they had just been released from prison, were wearing familiar-looking T-shirts. One had a picture of Bugs Bunny, the other Daffy Duck. Both shirts were decorated with silver sparkles, and they glinted in the train's fluorescent lights each time I turned my head.

Score another coup for my fashionable thirteen-year-old.

I work in a newsroom, and I sit near the fashion editor. I mentioned the cartoon characters festooned with sparkles to her and she confirmed that Looney Tunes are big. Apparently, this was old news, and I just wasn't paying attention. But how did Taz know about it before anybody else? It's not like he reads *Women's Wear Daily*. It's like this stuff comes to him in a dream.

One of his most persistent visions involved the North Face brand. He and his brother begged me for North Face jackets winter after winter, but I just couldn't see paying hundreds of dollars for outerwear that's designed to withstand polar cold when our worst winter weather rarely dips below twenty degrees.

Finally, we happened to come upon a North Face outlet while we were visiting Freeport, Maine, which is famous for its outlet stores. Since the jackets were all under a hundred bucks and both boys had outgrown their coats from the previous year, I agreed to buy them big black puffy parkas with hoods trimmed in fake gray fur.

Soon after I made these purchases, I mentioned them to a colleague who lives in the Northwest. He started laughing uproariously and said that North Face is aimed at trekkers and outdoor types, not urban kids.

But he was wrong. A few months later, on the first cold day that year, every single person I saw—young, old, fat, thin, black, white, male, female—was wearing a North Face jacket, except for me.

It was like I'd stepped into an alternate universe or a science fiction movie masquerading as an ad for North Face. I was in a hall of North Face mirrors, or a crazy dream. No matter which way I turned—in elevators, on street corners, waiting on line at the drugstore—there was the logo: THE NORTH FACE in all caps, next to three curved white stripes designed to evoke the cold mountaintops that wearing the brand will prepare you to climb. I was surrounded. Suddenly, I felt cold, very cold, in my sheepskin coat and woolen scarf.

That night, the temperature plunged. I had to walk

the dog before I could go to bed. It was chilly in our apartment, and I really didn't feel like making myself even more miserable by going outside. My sheepskin coat was OK, but to stay warm outside on a night like this, I needed to layer a sweater underneath, and wrap a scarf around my head, and I'd still get chilled. Meanwhile, the dog was giving me her Sad-Eyed Lady of the Lowlands look. I sighed and got up to find my boots.

Then I saw Taz's North Face hanging on a hook by the front door. He was in his room, doing his homework. I slipped the jacket on, zipped it up, and put the leash on the dog. Quietly, I opened and shut the door, gave the dog her pre-bedtime stroll, and discreetly returned to the apartment. As I unzipped the jacket, Taz came out of his room.

"I didn't say you could borrow that," he said.

"I paid for it," I said defensively. "My money, my coat. And I only wore it around the block to walk the dog. Besides, I was cold. And it's really warm."

He smiled. "You shoulda bought one for you when we were in that store," he said.

"I shoulda," I conceded. "Shoulda, woulda, coulda— didn't." (I once heard Hillary Clinton say that in response to some accusation, and I've found it comes in very handy as a way to explain a great deal of human behavior.)

You've probably figured out by now that I'm the type of person who doesn't buy new clothes to stay in style. I buy new clothes when my old ones are so worn out that

I'm almost embarrassed to donate them to the Salvation Army.

It's not that I don't want to spend the money on new clothes, although, I admit, I am a cheapskate. It's just the way I—and lots of people I know—were brought up. I've only had three winter coats in the last thirty years, and I plan to get a lot more years out of the one I have now before I get another one. (And if I can keep sneaking Taz's North Face instead of wearing mine, I'll get even more years out of that sheepskin.)

Besides, I know what would happen if I were to buy a North Face jacket. They would immediately go out of style. My purchase would have the opposite effect of my son's. Instead of everyone suddenly starting to wear what I'm wearing, they would immediately abandon what I'm wearing. And then I'd have to get new coats for Taz and Sport in whatever Taz deemed the next big style to be.

Now granted, not every thirteen-year-old lives in New York City, where you can pick up the latest fashion trends just by standing on a street corner for fifteen minutes and watching trendy people go by. (Of course, this does not explain why these trends are invisible to me, but irresistible to Taz.)

But chances are, even if you live in a small town or a leafy suburb in some other part of the country, your kid is still way trendier than you will ever be. That's because starting at around age thirteen, kids become part of something I have come to regard as the Global Youth Style Conspiracy.

No one has to tell members of the GYSC what the styles are. They just know. Why do bare-legged girls wear boots in the summer? Why do boys wear hats indoors and short sleeves in winter? You can't know the answers to those questions if you are a parent, because parents are not part of the GYSC.

But I have concluded that the slightest differences in logos, necklines, and waistbands are part of an intricate GYSC code, a way that kids send signals to each other. These signals mark them as members of various tribes— nerds, jocks, thugs, preppies, slackers, freaks. And while the differences in style may seem small—sometimes even undetectable—to you, to members of the GYSC, those subtle tribal markings are as strict as uniforms.

To help me flesh out my theory on the GYSC, I consulted with some friends around the country on what their teens were wearing. An acquaintance in North Carolina asked his daughter Miana and her friend Katie what's popular with, as he put it, "their ilk," and a few moments later he forwarded me this e-mail: "Daddy, why are my friends 'ilk'? My friends aren't ilk, they're freaks. We wear tanks, Rainbows, camis, jean shorts, Bermudas, Hollister is big, label stores mostly, skater shoes (i.e. Vans, etnies, things like that), ripped things (shorts, jeans, khakis), messy buns for hair, side bangs as well, hair bands around the wrist; for safe keeping ya know, and that's pretty much it. We layer, it's all the rage. We also wear a lot of hoodies and zip-ups. Ta da, your window into teenage girl-dom/fashion. Don't forget the short, preppy mini skirts that the sluts wear. Yeah, I said sluts. Ha. Don't tell Mommy."

It took me about a half hour, using my trusty translator Google, to decipher her message. And in case you're as out of it as I am, allow me to enlighten you: Rainbows are flip-flops; Hollister is a brand that sells rather normal-looking clothes like T-shirts and jeans (even though all of the clothing pictured on its website is inexplicably scrunched up and wrinkled, as if it had been left in the dryer too long), and skater shoes are sneakers for skateboarders, with thick rubber soles, air pockets in the heel, and occasional wild print designs.

On to the next glimpse of adolescent cool. "My boy likes to dress like a stoner," a friend in a New England college town e-mailed me, "but with oversized pants (he likes these made of hemp) and boxers showing. The T-shirts are all of our old friends, the Dead, Jimi Hendrix, Bob Marley, The Who, etc. The hair is long or shaved all the way off, the sneakers are huge and not tied. No visible socks. A Hacky Sack or skateboard is usually attached in some way."

Not sure what a Hacky Sack is? Me neither. Again, I had to look that one up on Google. I think the easiest way to explain it is to compare it to the beanbags I used to play with as a kid. My mother used to sew them by the dozen with leftover scraps of fabric, and, yes, she actually filled them with dried beans or seeds. (I suppose that sounds like something out of *Little House on the Prairie,* but actually it happened in the 1960s in New York.)

Well, now they sell little beanbaggy thingies for about $13 (I guess no one's mother sews toys from scraps of fabric anymore) and they are called Hacky Sacks. (I guess it wouldn't be cool to call them beanbags.) The biggest difference is, you don't catch or throw them with your hands; you kick them and do all kinds of other fancy footwork to keep them aloft. The game is actually called "footbag" and sometimes kids stand around in a circle playing it.

Next I called on a friend in Spokane, Washington, who has three boys, to get his take on local styles. He said the oldest has "long cultivated a type of gangsta look, with the sideways fitted baseball cap, wild pattern T-shirts, really baggy shorts and pants and the tops of his boxer shorts showing." Sound familiar?

His middle son wears a lot of Nike-label clothes, listens to hip-hop stations, and talks like a rapper. The youngest of the guys is into "basketball and football jerseys with baggy mesh shorts that have lots of holes and are three sizes too big."

I'm considering asking this family if they'd care to adopt a fourth son, because clearly Taz could move to Spokane tomorrow and fit right in.

But the one thing I don't quite get about all these modes of adolescent fashion is that the clothes don't necessarily correlate with who you are. The jock look, I've noticed, is big even among kids who haven't been on a team since they were forced to take sides in second-grade dodgeball (before schools banned dodgeball because it was too dangerous).

And surfer-dude style—floral-print shirts, baggy shorts and flip-flops—isn't just for guys at Malibu. I've seen kids waiting for the subway dressed this way, with no surfboard in sight.

The hip-hop set, meanwhile, has been gravitating toward the prep-school look—polo shirts with collars and three buttons. The only difference is, the polo shirt that used to come in sedate solid colors now comes with wild stripes of pink and gold. I know this for a fact because, of course, Taz has just such a shirt.

The look I find most puzzling of all consists of plaid Bermuda shorts and a white undershirt with slip-on canvas shoes. Yes, a really trendy kid these days looks like your father did twenty-five years ago the day you wanted to kill yourself because the neighbors saw him dressed like that to mow the lawn.

But the GYSC is not just about clothes. It's a whole culture, a frame of reference that assures any two kids from anywhere have more in common with each other than your own kid has with you.

Not long ago we hosted a visiting student from Colombia who was Taz's age. We brushed up on our *Holas,* but that turned out be unnecessary. Our guest, Sebastian, spoke perfect English. Not only that, but he pretty much got off the plane from Medellín, came to our house, sat down in the living room, and started playing Halo. You would have thought he lived on the block instead of on another continent.

I had set the clock radio in the room where he was sleeping to the local Spanish music station, but after a day, he politely asked if he could change it. "I don't really like Latin music," he explained. Just like Taz, he liked hip-hop and pop.

I offered to take him to the museum of his choice, a Broadway show, or any other New York landmark he wanted to see. But all he wanted to do was go to Times Square. He was in New York for six days, and managed to get to Times Square on three of them. While he was there, he bought a skateboard in what he claimed—and Taz confirmed—was a famous skateboard store. I, of course, had no idea there even was such a thing as a famous skateboard store. How does a kid from South America know about a skateboard store in Times Square and I, a lifelong New Yorker, do not? You guessed it: GYSC.

Even in the small rural town where we vacation up in Maine, I've found evidence of the GYSC. One day, for example, I heard Taz and another kid singing a song as they paddled a little boat in our pond. How nice, I thought, what a great bonding experience. Two buddies, enjoying the great outdoors on a beautiful summer day, singing at the top of their lungs.

The song came wafting to me in bits and echoes from across the water. The two of them were pumping their fists in the air and cracking up as they chanted the words together. But what exactly were they singing? I cocked my head and took a few steps toward the shore to see if I could pick it up. I could barely make it out, but I heard something about "gin and juice."

When they got back to shore, I asked them what they were singing. They snorted their laughter and mumbled, "Nothing, nothing." I filed the tidbit away. Later, when I was back home in New York and sitting at a computer, the incident popped into my mind again, and I decided to consult my dearest friend and all-knowing helper, Google. I typed in "gin and juice," and was treated to the lyrics of a Snoop Dogg song:

*"Rollin' down the street, smokin' indo, sippin' on gin and juice."*

I had heard of Snoop Dogg, but not indo. Again, I asked Google, and was sent to a link in Urban Dictionary.com, which informed me that indo is a type of marijuana.

Well, isn't that charming? Here I was, thinking these two boys were out there breathing in the fresh air and singing some uplifting youth anthem like, I don't know, "Michael, Row Your Boat Ashore," and come to find out that they'd been reciting the lyrics to a song about booze and drugs.

Another day up in Maine, Taz was wearing a G-Unit T-shirt. Of course, the other kids up there know what G-Unit is, but one of the other parents did not. He innocently looked at the shirt and asked, "Gun it? Why does your shirt say 'Gun it'?"

I sympathized with his ignorance because I hadn't known what it was, either, until Taz told me. And in case, dear reader, you don't know, allow me to educate you. G-Unit is the name of 50 Cent's brand and record label. And in case you don't know who 50 Cent is, he is a rapper who is famous for having survived being shot nine times. His first name is pronounced "Fiddy."

If I thought about it for too long, I could get completely hysterical about the fact that my son listens to songs about gin and indo, and that he admires a guy who's been shot nine times.

But I try to put these things in perspective. I may be a Terrible Mother, but I try not to be a hypocrite. I grew up listening to "Lucy in the Sky with Diamonds" and "Let's Spend the Night Together" in an era when rockers died from drug overdoses practically every day. I know from experience that singing a song with degenerate lyrics does not necessarily turn you into a degenerate.

Or at least, so I tell myself. Deep down inside, I fear that it might be so, but I refuse to dwell too long on the possibility, because it would just be too awful.

Besides, although it might seem irrelevant, I also like to remind myself that Fine Upstanding Citizens are hard to come by. Perhaps Fiddy is just as decent a person as anyone who has lately inhabited, say, the White House. Is a rapper who has been shot nine times really any worse than a president lying about weapons of mass destruction, Watergate, or, for that matter, sexual relations with *that* woman?

So I think I'll just save my outrage for more important issues. Like why, for example, elementary school class picnics are always scheduled for smack in the middle of the day, when I'm at work.

I also try not to be outraged by what I perceive to be the unfair disappearance of the ugly duckling stage of adolescence. (Unfair because *I* had to suffer through it, so why shouldn't everyone?) It used to be that most kids were downright funny-looking until they were about sixteen. They had braces and pimples and little-kid haircuts, and they were so embarrassed by their height and their bumps and everything else that they slouched in an effort to hide.

But all of that is no more. Now orthodonture starts with nine-year-olds, before the teeth that need correcting have even finished growing in. I suppose there are sound dental theories behind this, but one of the results is that the "metal mouth" stage is already well behind them by the time they hit thirteen.

And maybe I'm imagining this, but it seems to me that most teenagers don't even have pimples anymore. Do they all have personal dermatologists? Are they all getting facials? Or do they just know more about buying acne cream and cleansers than we did?

Not only that, but kids now all seem to have perfect posture. When I was a teenager, our mothers and aunts and grandmas were always yelling at us to stand up straight. But when was the last time you heard someone tell a kid to stand up straight? We slouched and dressed in lumps and layers and sacks of clothes because we didn't want anyone to see how awful we looked. As far as I can tell, teenagers these days have nothing to hide. Instead they are all about "LOOK AT ME!" They want the world to admire them.

And why shouldn't they? They look like movie stars, with fabulous smiles, fabulous clothes, and fabulous hair. Sometimes when I see a group of adolescent girls hanging out somewhere I almost can't stand it. How did they get so perfect looking?

The other morning I saw five or six of them standing around wearing short, flouncy little skirts over capris, sleeveless camisole tops with their bra straps showing, and flat, round-toed slippers. They looked like Degas ballerinas, the *Little Dancer of 14 Years* come to life.

And their hair, all in ponytails, was shiny, straight, and clean.

But how is that possible? I distinctly remember that when I was thirteen, half the girls had dandruff, and the other half had oil slicks on their scalps. (Ever the iconoclast, I kept changing membership from one group to the other.) So how is it that only weird people have dandruff these days? I can only assume that shampoo has come a long way in thirty years, and teenagers, in particular, use a lot more of it than they used to.

And it's not just the girls who take good care of their hair. Even Taz—whose regular trips to the barber keep his hair at Marine-regulation length—primps his buzz cut to make sure the quarter-inch-long locks are just so. A tube of "Styling Spiking Glue," whatever that is, and bottles of "Mega Hold Style & Control Gel" and "Extreme Hold Sculpting Freeze Gel" are just a few of the products kept in our bathroom to achieve this look.

Not all kids are into looking clean and perfect, of course. As one father put it, "Half of them are obsessed with shopping for new clothes, but the other half never change their clothes." The rocker-grunge look still has its adherents, and the uniform for them is as rigid as for anyone else. These are the kids who aspire to become Goth concert roadies, not Victoria's Secret models.

Their clothes are tattered—on purpose, of course— and they are slovenly and unwashed as well. They like leather jackets and black clunky boots, and they appear to have more than their share of tattoos, piercings, and hair dyed in colors normally found on tropical parrots.

I worry about people who pay to have sharp objects inserted through their skin or who shave their heads or chop their hair into asymmetrical patterns. Did they not get enough love when they were little?

I take it personally whenever one of my boys threatens—or even idly suggests—that he might some-day want an earring, a tattoo, or a blue streak in his hair. "I don't have pierced ears, why should you?" I say. "Treat your body like a temple, not like Coney Island!"

Taz's response to this peculiar little aphorism of mine is usually "Whatever," but isn't it obvious what I mean? Don't put garish colors on yourself that look like a run-down amusement park ride! Don't mutilate your flesh like some freak in a sideshow! Don't treat your body like an ocean that people pee in or a beach that they litter with soda cans and cigarette butts!

At least cleanliness is not an issue with Taz. In fact, he's been known to shower multiple times in a day, and incessant changing of clothes has occasionally been a problem.

It's happened any number of times that I'll do the laundry after, say, four days, expecting to find four days' worth of dirty underwear, socks, and shirts from all four members of our family. But as I'm sorting and folding, making piles of clean clothes on the bed for each of us, I'll notice that there are eight or nine pairs of pants for Taz, and as many as a dozen shirts. He has apparently been changing clothes three times a day, or perhaps he's changed into evening wear upon his arrival home from school.

Unfortunately, I sometimes have the opposite problem with Sport. For the preadolescent in the household, the pile of laundry is often troublingly small. There might be one or two pairs of socks in there for the entire week, along with a shirt and pants so filthy that they need to go through the wash again. But he'll be thirteen soon enough, and I don't see him going grunge. Sport already has a taste for boxers and fancy sneakers, so changing clothes three times a day shouldn't be far behind.

I just hope that Taz, when he grows up, isn't stuck in the fashion of his youth. I mean, if Jordans instantly mark you as old-fashioned in the year 2027, I hope he can move on to something more appropriate.

And in this respect, I hope he does not emulate his mother. To this day, my pants must brush the tops of my shoes or I feel embarrassed. I just cannot bear to wear short pants. When cropped pants and capris came back into style for women, I really couldn't wear them. I just kept thinking, every time I saw them, "Highwater, highwater, where's the flood?"

# CONSULTING THE EXPERTS

**W**hen my children were little, I consulted all kinds of reference books. *Your Baby & Child,* by Penelope Leach, whom I think of as a British Dr. Spock, was my favorite. I loved reading her advice about how to entertain a baby: "Try putting him in a carriage under a tree or where he can see patterns of light and shade or perhaps a line full of dancing washing." Not that my children would be happy for more than thirty seconds lying in their carriage under a tree without screaming their heads off, but it was such a lovely fantasy to imagine spending the afternoon that way.

Then there was her advice on how to feed a toddler: "Above all, try to get him used to eating cheese. Bread or crackers with cheese and a tomato or an apple is a perfectly balanced meal."

This is exactly what I would love to eat three times a day! Unfortunately, my children prefer Go-GURTs and Lunchables.

But once my boys were past diapers, I could no longer pretend that Penelope's wholesome ideas were working. My kids were more *Where the Wild Things Are* than *Winnie the Pooh*. Besides, I later found out that Penelope had had an unhappy childhood—she was often separated from her parents, who eventually divorced and sent her to boarding school—and I realized she was probably living in a fantasy world.

But I didn't give up on the experts; I merely branched out. First, I tried reading all the books about *The (Fill-in-the-Blank) Child.* There was a book called *Raising Your Spirited Child,* another titled *The Sensitive Child,* and one called *The Challenging Child,* along with *The Difficult Child,* and *Your Gifted Child.* I read the sleep book, the food book, and the all-about-boys book. I read about how to raise a moral child, a drug-free child, a wealthy child, a respectful child, a joyous child, and a TV-free child. (Not that I had any intention of getting rid of television—are you kidding? It was the only peace and quiet I ever got, when the kids were watching television.)

I then moved on to books about intelligence— *Emotional Intelligence, Social Intelligence, Multiple Intelligences,* and every other kind of intelligence except military intelligence—all of which made me keenly feel my own lack of intelligence. If only I could figure out whether Taz was best described as logical or people-oriented? Musical or visual? And what about me? Was I like the mother in *Slummy Mummy,* or was I more like the author of *Confessions of a Slacker Mom?* Most of the time I just felt like the Clueless Mom.

Reading about all these different categories didn't exactly solve my problems, but at least they made me feel less weird. I figured if I could find a chapter in every book that described some aspect of my child, then whatever was going on in our house was probably normal.

For example, it was sort of a relief to find out I wasn't the only mother with a kid who refused to wear pajamas because "they feel funny." At first I saw this as a problem, and I tried many different types of pajamas made from various fabrics in an effort to identify an acceptable brand. But I finally gave up, after reading in one book that there are some children so sensitive to the way things feel that they only like wearing very soft clothes.

Reading that made it OK, somehow, and his rejection of pajamas actually turned out to be something of a blessing. Both he and his brother got used to sleeping in whatever T-shirt or jersey they were planning to wear the next day, and that made getting dressed in the morning quicker.

It was only later that I learned that pajamas as sleepwear aren't considered cool anymore. But pajamas as streetwear—well, that's a whole different story. Kids don't want to wear them to bed when they're four, but they don't mind wearing them to school when they're thirteen.

Somehow, the small comforts I had gotten from reading books about raising young children did not carry over to reading books about raising adolescents. One look at the table of contents in *Parenting Teens with Love & Logic,* with chapter headings called "Sex" and "Drug or Substance Abuse," made me want to turn to the chapter called "Suicide Threats" and make a few of those myself. The chapter titled "Parties," I could only guess, had nothing to do with tips for making your own piñata.

Actually, there was one passage in that book that was unintentionally hilarious. It was in the section on how not to let kids yank your chain by overreacting to provocative statements they might make. As an example, the authors offered the hypothetical scenario of a parent asking, "What if my kid comes home and says something off the wall, like, communism is a really great way to distribute wealth and create just societies? How do I handle that?"

This cracked me up because the only person in our house who would ever say something like that is Elon. Now, don't go thinking I'm some left-wing lunatic or anything; I assure you I am not. I leave the left-wing stuff to him, and in return he doesn't follow me into the voting booth. He also allows me to invest in the stock market even though it is, in his view, a pillar of a corrupt capitalist society. (When we retire, however, and find that there is no dacha waiting for us in the Russian countryside, I suspect we will be thanking our 401(k)s for allowing us to dine on something other than 9Lives.)

In contrast, Taz, like a lot of materialistic, money-obsessed kids his age, is the Ultimate Capitalist. He imagines some future life where he'll be living in a mansion with a pool (unlike our cramped apartment), driving a nice car (anything would be nicer than our twenty-year-old junkheap with 130,000 miles on it), and eating takeout every night (instead of my strict "we can only afford to eat out once a week").

I remind him, of course, that in order to achieve the lordly existence of his dreams, one must have a *rawther* high-paying job, and those jobs don't tend to be handed to people who failed to graduate from high school. But, naturally, he finds that part of the discussion to be unutterably boring.

He also can't seem to accept the concept of cutting back on consumption in order to keep expenses down. I'm forever yelling at him and Sport to turn off the lights and the TV when they leave the room, not just to save the earth, but, more important, to save on the electric bill.

When I was a kid, if you left the light on, somebody's mother would always say, "Whaddaya, got stock in the electric company?"

But when I tried that line on Taz, he said, "That's a good idea! Can we get some stock in the electric company? And maybe we should get some stock in Starbucks, too? And Apple?"

The authors of that guide to raising teenagers, with their example of a kid advocating communism in order to shock you, seem not to have anticipated the possibility that your kids might be more conservative politically than you are. But they do offer an all-purpose line to use—whatever your obnoxious adolescent's viewpoint might be. When he voices an opinion that challenges your values and everything you hold dear, you just say, "Thanks for sharing that. I've always wondered how teenagers see that."

So I told Elon that if Taz decided to pick a fight with him by saying that he idolizes Donald Trump or some other (in Elon's view) capitalist pig-dog, we should simply say, "Thanks for sharing," and smile.

But it never worked out that way. Any time Taz expressed admiration for someone on the order of Paris Hilton, neither Elon nor I could contain our horror. Like every other parent who ever existed, we instead wasted our breath trying to explain to our child why his adulation for someone we had no respect for was not only upsetting but also morally bankrupt.

To which Taz would usually respond, "Whatever."

It struck me as incredibly ironic that we couldn't let things go with a simple "Thank you for sharing," but he had no problem dismissing us with "Whatever." I wonder sometimes if he hasn't been secretly reading a book called *A Teenager's Guide to Blowing Off Parents*.

One question that I didn't find the answer to in the guide to raising teens is why, once my child turned thirteen, did he decide that he could not spend more than five minutes in his own house? For years, my living room was the default location for entire gangs of neighborhood boys. They would play video games, have Stephen King movie marathons, and pig out on junk food for hours while camping out on my sofa and floor. From the time Taz was eleven to the time he officially became a teenager, it seemed like no weekend went by without my hosting at least a half-dozen boys for a meal or two.

Sport loved having all these big boys around. He made a pest of himself most of the time, but they were, for the most part, very good-natured about including him in their football games, their video games, and even their movie watching, though we had to drag him out of the room when the Jim Carrey or Eddie Murphy videos gave way to *Pet Sematary*. (Sport was so enamored of the big guys that I finally had to institute a rule: You can't invite anyone to your birthday party who is more than twice your age.)

For a while there, it felt like I was running the Harpaz Hilton, or an overnight camp for middle schoolers. They were big enough so that they didn't mind sleeping in their clothes, and they were too old to wake up in the middle of the night and demand to be taken home, the way they sometimes do when they're little. But they were also small enough that two or three of them could sleep on the pullout sofa bed, another one could curl up in the big armchair, and another two could manage on a blow-up mattress on the floor.

Every now and then one of my neighbors would peek her head in the apartment and be horrified by the large number of boys she saw there.

"I don't know how you can stand it," she'd say.

But I was thrilled that Taz had such nice friends. They even berated Taz if he was fresh to me. "Don't talk to your mother like that!" one of them would inevitably say. In fact, in many ways, they were utterly unlike what I had expected adolescent boys to be. They made eye contact, they said hello, they brought their dirty dishes into the kitchen. Some of them—but by no means all— even put the seat down after using the toilet.

When I was in second grade, my teacher had us write down our dreams for when we grew up, and I remember writing that I wanted to have twelve children. Well, I only had two of my own, but some days it felt like I was the den mother for the whole dozen.

But something changed when Taz turned thirteen. My living room was suddenly empty. No more movie marathons. Saturday night no longer included a moment around 3 a.m. when I would have to go out and tell them to shut up and go to sleep for God's sake, before I called their parents. Sunday mornings no longer involved making bacon and eggs for a crowd.

Instead, Taz was just never home. Here is a typical exchange between the two of us if he was kind enough to stop by and drop off his book bag before heading out again five minutes later.

ME: Where are you going?
HIM: Places.
ME: But who are you going with?
HIM: Oh you know—peeps.

(Presumably, dear reader, you are sufficiently in the know to realize that this refers not to a type of marshmallowy Easter candy shaped like baby chickens, but is thug-talk for the word *people,* as in "my peeps.")

ME: And what exactly are you planning to do with
    these . . . peeps?
HIM: I don't know. Like, chill, prolly?

(Note: "Prolly" is not a girl's name. It is teenage mumblespeak for "probably." You will find it on page 34 of the book I intend to write for Berlitz one day called *Useful Phrases for Touring the Adolescent Countryside.*)

Later, if I would I call him on his cell and ask what he was doing, he would tell me: "Jus' chillin'."

Well. Natch!

Sometimes days would go by without a single Taz sighting.

"I'm sleeping over at Ethan's," he'd say in a call Friday night.

"Tonight I'll be at Michael's," the word would come Saturday night.

I didn't know whether to put him on the endangered

species list or issue an AMBER Alert. He'd leave messages on the answering machine from time to time, and sometimes he'd come home to change clothes, which I deduced from the fact that his dirty laundry pile kept growing even when no one had slept in his bed.

Often on Sunday nights, though, he'd make an appearance. Why?

"I have a twenty-page paper due on *The Odyssey*. I forgot to read it, and it's due tomorrow."

When I thought back to those days of having all those boys camping out in our living room, it made me sad. I hadn't changed, so what was different? Couldn't they just please land on me all of a sudden for dinner one night, like the old days? I told myself if only they'd all have another movie marathon, I wouldn't even complain about the smelly feet. I wouldn't even yell at them to be quiet if they woke me up with their hollering at 3 a.m.!

I offered to cater Chinese food, if only Taz would invite a bunch of his friends over. They could even order a pay-per-view wrestling event on the TV in my bedroom and leave potato chip crumbs on my pillows!

But no matter what I offered, Taz was having none of it. "That's OK," he'd say in a singsong voice on his way out the door. "See ya!"

When I finally got him to explain himself, he said his friends had just gotten too big for our little living space. They were six feet tall now, not five feet tall. They couldn't sleep curled up in the living room chair anymore. He couldn't even hang out in his own room with a couple of friends; it was barely big enough for a single bed, a dresser, and a nightstand. The only air conditioner and cable TV was in the bedroom I shared with Elon. How could he invite six big guys over to watch a show in his mother's bedroom?

I had to agree, when I thought about it, that that would be awkward. Even hanging out in our living room was problematic. Any noise made in one room could be heard in all the rooms. They wanted to stay up late without having a mother come and shush them, and they wanted to play video games and watch movies without having a little brother interrupt them.

Our lack of physical space had never been an issue before. We had three small bedrooms, a living room/dining room, and a kitchen. Sure, there were always kids' toys all over the place, and homework got done at the dining-room table next to the computer desk, but I never felt deprived.

Once when the place was being repainted, we all had to live in the master bedroom together for a week. I actually kind of liked it. It was cozy. Simple. A little crowded, yes, but not unmanageable. It made me realize that if I had to live in Japan, in one of those tiny little spaces with the screens and the beds that you roll up, I'd be totally fine.

Besides, I hate housekeeping. I figured the fewer rooms, the less vacuuming. I didn't mean to create a Spartan existence for my family, but I always felt like it was just the right amount of space. One bathroom for four people never bothered us, though on that count, I considered myself lucky to have boys, who rarely spend more than thirty seconds in the bathroom at a time, anyway.

But now I tried to see it through Taz's eyes. For the first time, I wished I had a big house with a basement, or a den, or a family room or playroom, where Taz and his buddies could sprawl. I had no place to put a Ping-Pong table or a dartboard. And since I couldn't offer any of that, Taz said I'd just have to get used to the fact that he was going to hang out elsewhere.

One of his friends had a big-screen TV, cable, and central air in a media room; his mom was happy to have Taz over any time. Another friend was an only child with an entire floor at his disposal and plenty of room for other kids to sleep over. Another kid had a country house at a lake, and spending the weekend there was far preferable in Taz's eyes to sitting at home playing Monopoly with me and his little brother.

Taz managed to go to swankier places, too. One of his friends' parents had a beach house in the Hamptons. I'd just like to announce that I have never been to the Hamptons. I have never even been invited to the Hamptons. But there was one weekend last summer where not only was Taz in the Hamptons, but my niece was in the Hamptons, too, and they weren't even together. They both, and let me stress here, separately, had people to visit in the Hamptons. My sister and I did not. "Yes," I e-mailed her that weekend, "we ARE chopped liver!"

One weekend while Taz was chillin' in the Hamptons, I happened to pick up the Sunday *New York Times*. In a column in the back of the magazine, Marion Winik, a mother about my age, bemoaned her sixteen-year-old son's unwillingness to spend more than five minutes at home. On that rare occasion when he deigned to drop by, he told her it was only to pick up his fifteen-year-old stepbrother so that they could go "chill at Trav's."

"What exactly is involved in 'chilling at Trav's' I will leave to your imagination—God knows it's had a vivid dramatic life in mine," she wrote. She denied permission for the outing, which was followed, she said, by "shock, outrage and furious debate. The main arguments they offered were that they are teenagers, it is summer and I am stupid." Later that night, the boys sneaked out of the house. She located them by cell phone, ordered them home, and they argued some more.

Well, at least I was not alone in wondering why my house is the last place my son would care to be at any given moment. But reading Winik's column had made me depressed. I actually hadn't allowed my imagination to consider the many things Taz might be doing when he claimed to be "chillin'" with "peeps." I had in the past expressed concern about some of the less-savory types who hang out along the main drag in our neighborhood, but he assured me they were no problem.

"You mean those people drinkin' forties and smoking cigarettes down on the corner?" Taz asked. "Don't worry about them, they know me."

Was that supposed to make me feel better? It didn't.

I have an old collection of Erma Bombeck's humor columns that I pick up now and then in an effort to comfort myself when I start worrying too much about the fact that I Am a Terrible Mother. I read the book kind of like how my boys liked to have me read *The Runaway Bunny* over and over again to them when they were little.

"If you run away," the mommy bunny told her little bunny, "I will run after you." No matter where the little bunny goes, the mommy bunny finds him. But now that my bunny was a great big bunny, there was no hunting him down. I remembered Erma had tackled this subject at some point; I flipped through the book and found it.

"In my mind, I always dreamed of the day I would have teenagers," she wrote. She imagined that they'd all gather around the piano and sing songs together, then have a family meeting to decide on what flavor ice cream they were going to have.

"It never worked out that way," she added. "Our teenagers withdrew to their bedrooms on their thirteenth birthday and didn't show themselves to us again until it was time to get married. If we spoke to them in public, they threatened to self-destruct within three minutes."

She also had these words of wisdom: "Could I have

ever comprehended that something so simple, so beautiful and so uncomplicated as a child could drive you to shout, 'We are a family and you're a part of this family, and by God, you're going to spend a Friday night with us having a good time if we have to chain you to the bed!' "

Well, it was a relief to know I was in good company and that this problem of children who disappear at age thirteen was not unique to my family, but had existed way back in the middle of the last century—a term I love to use because it upsets my sister. She read a reference recently to something that happened in the middle of the last century, and it took her a few minutes to realize that they were talking about the decade she grew up in and not something out of Dickens.

Reading Erma calmed me down enough that I could face a stiffer dose of advice—from my old friend and oracle Google. I figured I ought to read up on some serious subjects now that itchy pajamas were no longer my main concern. So I screwed up my courage and went surfing for wisdom on adolescents and marijuana—or should I say *weed,* which is the term most teenagers prefer these days.

But most of the websites I found sounded like they were either written by Joe Friday from the old TV series *Dragnet* ("Marijuana is the flame! Heroin is the fuse! LSD is the bomb!") or by Bob Marley. The websites offered by the government were the scariest. A study from the Substance Abuse and Mental Health Services Administration (Did you know we have such a thing? Your tax dollars, hard at work!) told me that "those who used marijuana weekly were nine times as likely as nonusers to say they use alcohol or drugs . . . six times as likely to say they had run away from home . . . nearly six times as likely to say they had cut classes or skipped school . . . five times as likely to say they stole."

OK, it's one thing if your kid tries pot—er, weed—but according to this, he's also going to run away from home, skip school, and become a thief.

The scariest study was what I like to call the Reefer Madness study, by British doctors, which claimed to show an increase in psychosis among people who smoke pot. The study appeared to be valid and scientific and built upon many other reputable studies.

But the researchers admitted that they couldn't be sure that smoking was causing the psychosis. Maybe, instead, people who are in early stages of psychosis feel the need to go out and smoke. This reminded me of my long-held conviction that all heroin addicts start out by drinking milk.

Reading about the study inspired me to want to see the movie *Reefer Madness* and actually watch some pot smokers lose their minds. My ever-reliable Window on the Universe, Google, obliged. Turns out *Reefer Madness* can be seen its in entirety on Google Video because it's in the public domain. The film was originally made in the 1930s as an anti-marijuana propaganda movie, but it became a cult film in the seventies after being rediscovered in the Library of Congress by a guy who advocates the decriminalization of marijuana. The movie's pot smokers grin maniacally, are horny as hell, and dance a lot at parties, reminding me of teenagers in general, whether they smoke pot—or weed, or whatever—or not.

As long as I was investigating the subject, I decided to check out an article on another website, titled "Marijuana: Telling Teenagers the Truth About Smoking Pot," which was more or less at the other end of the spectrum.

"Pot is less addictive than coffee," the article states. Its author does admit that "pot will cause some short-term memory loss," but reassuringly notes that it's no more serious than the memory loss caused by beer. Risks to pot smokers, according to the website, include gaining weight because of the munchies and having too much sex.

The author adds, "I have been smoking pot for the last twenty-five years and I still test as a genius on IQ tests."

The Genius goes on to point out that pot is illegal, and you could go to jail if you get caught with it.

"People get very weird about pot," he notes. "So if anyone asks if you've been smoking pot, Just Say No!"

At the Partnership for a Drug-Free America website, I decided to take the "Two-Minute Challenge." Embarrassingly, I only got two of the eight questions right (whether cigarette use among teens is down—yes; and whether sniffing powdered heroin is risky—yes, or should I say, duh). All the tricky questions—where do most kids get their drugs (the right answer is friends, while I guessed classmates), and where most kids get information about drugs (school, not, as I guessed, the media)—I flubbed.

Then I decided to do a little research into the oft-repeated notion that eating dinner together with your family is the key to raising perfect children. Turns out this comes from a survey by the National Center on Addiction and Substance Abuse at Columbia University. The survey found that the more often children eat dinner with their families, the less likely they are to smoke, drink, or use drugs.

One of the differences between researching things on Google and reading a book is that when you read a book, you get the author's point of view, and all the evidence he has gathered to support his point of view. But when you research a topic on Google, you get every point of view. So virtually every study you turn up, the results are countered by the next link.

In this case, the next page I clicked on took me to an academic's analysis that convinced me the survey about family dinners was hopelessly flawed. Eating dinner together, the analysis said, is a sign that a family is already functioning well. It's an effect, not a cause. The analysis went so far as to say that a screwed-up family that starts eating dinner together will probably make its children even more screwed up than they already are.

We do eat dinner together most nights, but then

again, I think we're pretty loopy as families go, so according to this analysis, I was just making my kids turn out worse by sitting at the dinner table with them.

By the way, did you ever notice how often in *The Sopranos* Tony and Carmela sat down with their kids for dinner like a normal family? Not just that famous last scene in the diner, mind you, but lots of times at home, they'd gather together for a meal. Now, if that isn't proof that a dysfunctional family only makes their children more dysfunctional by eating together, what is?

Actually, Elon and I had some wonderful parental bonding moments watching Tony and Carmela argue about their children. In fact, I would count *The Sopranos* among my sources for child-rearing information—if only as a reality check on my own life.

One of my favorite episodes was when Meadow and a bunch of other teenagers threw a party with booze and drugs in her grandmother's house, trashing the place. Tony fetched Meadow and brought her home, and Carmela asked him what he said to their daughter.

TONY: I don't know. I yelled. What the fuck else am I going to do?

CARMELA: There have to be consequences. What kind of parents would we be if we let her get away with it?

TONY: Typical.

CARMELA: Plenty of parents still crack the whip.
TONY: Yeah. That's what they *tell* ya.

At this point in the show, Elon and I looked at each other. That's *exactly* what Taz says! He's always claiming that nobody else's parents really punish them—they just *say* they punish them to save face in front of other parents!

Later, as Tony and Carmela tried to figure out some way to make Meadow pay for her crimes, Tony told Carmela: "If she finds out we're powerless, we're fucked."

It was delicious to see that Tony, who could whack people without a second thought, who was swift and unmerciful when it came to punishing anyone who challenged him, was completely hamstrung by his teenage child.

In the end, they punished Meadow by taking away her credit card. For three weeks.

Taz doesn't have a credit card yet, but the offers come daily in the mail. This, too, is completely alien to me. Like a lot of people my age, my parents didn't have any credit cards when I was a kid. My dad finally got one in the seventies when car-rental companies stopped accepting cash. I remember getting my first one after I'd been out of college and working full-time for a few years. It was a really big deal; I felt so honored that American Express deemed me worthy of their trust!

Little did I know that twenty years later, I'd be on the phone with their service center, begging them to stop clogging my mailbox with offers for more cards. At lower rates! With cash advances! And extra cards for everyone in the family—even my children!

Maybe Meadow Soprano needed a credit card, but Taz does not.

There was one other type of show that I thought might help my dysfunctional family in my search for expert advice. I tried watching, with my children, all the shows about the mean nannies who come in and straighten out screwed-up families.

But I could never bear to watch through to the end. It was just all too close to home—the spoiled children, the household in chaos, the clueless grown-ups. Besides, it always seemed to me that no matter what the circumstances were, the nanny always blamed the mother.

Usually by the time that scene was about to unfold, where the nanny would confront the mother about how everything was all her fault, I would be near tears and would beg the kids to change the channel. I just couldn't bear watching a fellow Terrible Mother's public humiliation.

Then one day I came up with the brilliant idea of applying to be on one of the nanny shows. I didn't want to watch the humiliation scene, but somehow the idea of being part of it was appealing (in an anorexia-bulimia kind of a way).

I located the show's website—naturally—by Googling it.

"Kids driving you nuts?" the website asked. "Need harmony at home?"

Yes! Yes! I filled out the application form and e-mailed it in. I mentioned to a colleague at work that I had done this, thinking that it was a very clever thing to do, but he looked at me like I was out of my mind.

"Did you tell your family that you are doing this? Does Elon know?"

Well, no, I thought I'd surprise them.

Next thing I knew, I got an e-mailed response, thanking me for my query, and instructing me on how to submit a video of household chaos so that they could make sure we would be a good fit for the show.

The only problem was, the only person in the family who was capable of making a video was Taz, but how could he make the video if the video was supposed to show him out of control? I decided to let Elon in on my little surprise and ask his advice about the video.

Up until this point, I had, as my colleague at work pointed out, neglected to inform Elon that I had nominated our family to be on one of the nanny shows. And I have to admit, I was not prepared for the vehemence of his reaction.

"You did WHAT? Are you out of your MIND? No, I'm not going to help you figure out how to make a video of our so-called household chaos, and if you figure it out on your own, I'm telling you right now that I refuse to have any part in anything that happens thereafter!"

Maybe calling in a TV nanny for help wasn't such a good idea if it was going to cause my divorce.

I abandoned the idea, and went back to reading books. Someone told me that Nora Ephron's *I Feel Bad About My Neck* had a section on raising children, so I thought perhaps that would be both amusing and instructive. Well, it was funny, and I did laugh. Even the author photo was hilarious—surely the most memorable author photo of all time, with her hiding her neck, and half of her face, under a black turtleneck pulled up all the way to her eyeballs.

Then I got to the chapter on parenting, which Nora started off by pointing out that when her kids were young, "you didn't need a book" to tell you how to be a parent.

Well, Nora, I said to myself, you must have been a parent somewhere in the middle of the last century, because I definitely need lots of books, including, apparently, yours.

Nowadays, the book continued, people who engage in the practice of "parenting," which also apparently did not exist in the middle of the last century, have been told that "if your children believed you understood them, or at least tried to understand them, they wouldn't hate you when they became adolescents."

I had to admit she was right. That was part of why it was so awful that Taz no longer wanted anything to do with us. We were foolish enough to think that unlike with our own parents, there was no generation gap here. We thought we understood what being a teenager was all about. But Taz thought otherwise.

"Your adolescent is sullen. Your adolescent is angry. Your adolescent is mean," Nora added. "Your adolescent is probably smoking marijuana, which you may have smoked too, but not until you were at least eighteen. Your adolescent is undoubtedly having completely inappropriate and meaningless sex, which you didn't have until you were in your twenties, if then."

By then I was feeling nauseous. This was much more upsetting than any of the nanny shows.

She went on to point out that parents who engage in "parenting" have devoted themselves to their children in every way—emotionally, materially, and physically. And yet, she said, adolescents still turn out "exactly the way adolescents have always turned out. Only worse."

I knew I was supposed to be laughing at this, but I wasn't. It was too shocking to be funny. How could she know these things? How could she be so wise, she who raised her children in the middle of the last century when there was no such thing as parenting?

I put the book down on my lap and I stared at the ceiling.

My mind was racing.

The immortal words of another expert on child rearing suddenly popped into my head.

"If you bungle raising your children, nothing else much matters in life."

You could say a lot of things about Jackie Kennedy. But you could never say that she was a Terrible Mother.

## ANOTHER CALL
## FROM SCHOOL

*T*he phone rang at my desk at work. I glanced nervously at the caller ID. Just as I'd feared, it was Taz's school.

Again.

"Hi, this is the social studies teacher. We had another incident today."

"Really?" My heart was pounding. I reminded myself about being a Terrible Mother. "I'm sorry," I said. "I hope it wasn't too serious. What happened?"

"Well," said the teacher, "this time he brought a can of soda to class."

Oh my God, I thought, a can of soda, what horrible things could he have done with a can of soda? He probably threw it at the teacher and blinded her in one eye! Or maybe he dumped it on another kid's head and the other boy took out a knife and stabbed him! Or else he spilled it on the computer that houses the server for the entire New York City Board of Education and the records for all 1 million students have been erased!

I screwed up my courage to continue the conversation. "And . . . what happened?"

"Well," said the teacher, "I asked him to throw the can away."

I was almost afraid to go on, but I forced myself. "And?"

"And he wouldn't."

"I'm not following you," I said. "He brought the soda to class. And you asked him to throw it away because . . .?"

"Because it's against the rules!" she said impatiently. "*Completely* against the rules! They're not allowed to bring any food, or drink, to class."

It seemed like a dumb rule to me. I mean, who cares if a kid brings a can of soda to class? But then, I'm ashamed to admit that like a lot of Americans, I've gotten totally addicted to never being without something to eat or drink for more than fifteen seconds, and apparently I'd raised Taz to be the same way.

I realized this would not be the right time to make excuses for my child's behavior, nor would it have been appropriate to debate whether the rule is a good one or not. This call was a dressing-down for being a Terrible Mother, and I was just going to have to sit there quietly and take it.

"I see," I said in my most humble and polite tone of voice. "So he brought the can of soda to class, and that's against the rules. And then what happened?"

"Well," she said, in her by now unbearably slow

95

delivery of a course of events so earth-shattering that she had to call me at work, "the whole class stopped."

She wasn't exactly reeling me in with compelling details here. I noticed that my mood was starting to change from guilt and proactive horror at my evil son's doings, to annoyance at being interrupted at my desk. I may be a Terrible Mother, but I had work to do! Deadlines to meet! Stuff that was way more important than listening to a blow-by-blow description of how my son's soda can somehow brought down the entire system of education in the United States of America.

"OK," I finally said, trying not to sound too impatient, "and THEN what happened?"

"Well, that was it. I asked him to throw it away, and he refused, and the class just stopped."

I was trapped in a cartoon with five possible captions, but I couldn't bring myself to say any of them. So I just said them in my head:

"The entire class came to a halt because he had a can of *soda?*"

"What if he threw a chair?"

"What if *you had ignored the entire incident and gone on teaching?*"

"What would you have done if he had a *gun?*"

"Every time a kid breaks a rule, do you call his mother?"

The words kept bouncing inside my brain like the refrain of a top forty song, but they never came out of my mouth. Finally, I apologized for my son's behavior and promised to talk to him about it. I gave the teacher permission to impose whatever punishment she deemed appropriate. I thanked her for calling, and hung up.

A few minutes later the phone rang again. I looked at the caller ID. The school.

I got up from my desk and walked away. The phone went silent after the third ring; the answering machine kicked in, confirming what I and the person on the other end already knew: I Am a Terrible Mother.

Later, I mentioned the incident to a friend, thinking she'd have a good laugh with me about it. I imagined myself chuckling as I said, "Can you imagine how ridiculous that is? The teacher couldn't deal with a kid who brought a can of soda to class?"

But instead, as soon as I started to tell the story, my friend gasped in horror.

"Oh my GOD!" she said. "Are you KIDDING ME?? He brought a can of SODA to class? You can't just break the RULES like that! You're going to have to think up some REALLY bad punishment for this one!"

What I felt like saying was: "Gee, maybe I could take his nonexistent credit card away for three weeks?" But, of course, I didn't say that. In fact, at this point in our conversation, I wished I were about two inches tall and that I could disappear. I heard myself stuttering, which is something I almost never do, as I tried to quickly come up with some type of appropriate answer.

"Ah, yeh-yeh-yes, um, I, I was just, just thinking that,

d-d-definitely, I'm really going to have to t-t-talk to T-taz about this," I said, before declaring that I was so thirsty I needed to get a soda—I'd been at least five minutes without something to drink. Then I slunk away.

The soda incident was hardly the first time Taz got in trouble with a teacher. He was a wild little boy in the early years of elementary school. He didn't want to sit still. He didn't want to do his homework. He just wanted to play and play and play. When he was in kindergarten, I got a call from school one day saying that he had simply up and left the building.

Fortunately, a passerby found him on a nearby street corner, apparently headed home, and returned him to the school just as his teacher was realizing he'd disappeared.

"What were you thinking?" I said when I picked him up that day.

"School is too boring, Mommy," he explained. "I didn't want to stay there anymore."

I smothered an impulse to say, "Welcome to the real world, buddy! Everything in life feels that way some-times, but you just gotta do your time." After all, he was only five. I didn't want to break it to him yet that his best years were already behind him.

In fact, his feeling that school was kinda boring didn't change too much as the years wore on, although he knew better than to go AWOL in the middle of class. His favorite subject was recess; calls or notes home from the teacher were not unusual. He liked to fool around;

he wouldn't concentrate. He claimed frequent stomachaches, sore throats, twisted ankles—anything that might get him a day off. Parent-teacher night was my most dreaded night of the year, every year.

I finally consulted our pediatrician, a wise man whom I privately regard as the medical equivalent of King Solomon. Although he doesn't have a beard, I think of him stroking his beard as he contemplates my questions, which over the years have ranged from "Are you sure he doesn't have leukemia?" to "Isn't he done growing yet?"

What's especially good about this doctor is that he could be counted on to give sage advice for things that really didn't have a lot to do with medical care, such as "How do I deal with a kid who pretends to be sick so he doesn't have to go to school?"

"It's simple," the doctor said. "If he's not throwing up, if he doesn't have a fever, and if he doesn't have diarrhea, well, then, he has to go to school."

I laid down the doctor's rule, and that was the end of the "My tummy hurts" game. If only everything about raising children were that simple!

Fortunately, when Taz first got to middle school, we saw a huge change in his attitude. The middle school had an emphasis on science and technology, and he loved experimenting with dry ice, counting bacteria, and learning how to make PowerPoint presentations. He'd never liked reading, and I still couldn't get him much interested in that, but at least he was enjoying a lot of his classes.

But it took a long time for it to register with me and Elon how much better Taz was doing in sixth grade than he had been in elementary school. We steeled ourselves for the first (and always dreaded) parent-teacher conference of middle school, but to our astonishment, one teacher after another came up to us and told us how wonderful our son was.

"Taz is an extraordinary boy," his science teacher gushed. "He sets a wonderful example for the other students."

Elon and I looked at each other incredulously.

"Are you sure you're talking about *our* son?" Elon asked. "Maybe you have him confused with some other kid named Taz?"

Just as she was about to remind us that there is no other kid named Taz, the real Taz happened to be passing through the hallway. He was on his way to help out at the table where kids were selling cookies and juice as a fund-raiser for the PTA.

"Hello Mrs. L!" he said cheerily to the teacher. "How are you today? Nice to see you!"

Mrs. L beamed. "See what I mean?" she said to us. "He's just wonderful. It's a lovely reflection on his parents."

Taz's father and I were dumbfounded by this display. We were even more amazed to see his name on the list of top ten students in his grade that quarter. He immediately engaged in a contest with a couple of the other kids on the list to see who would be the highest achiever the next quarter.

This was completely contrary to everything he'd ever done in elementary school. Taz at the top of the class? Taz setting a good example for others? Taz adding up the points taken off his chemistry test to make sure the teacher calculated his grade properly? He'd undergone a total transformation.

The first half of middle school was also a good time for him socially. The boys he competed with academically were all sweet kids from nice families, and they spent a lot of time hanging out together. I got to know their parents; we kept in touch by phone and e-mail, saw each other at school functions, and occasionally compared notes. This was the gaggle of boys I mentioned earlier, who made our living room their second home sometimes, hanging out for dinner, video games, and sleepovers after school and on weekends.

The phone rang often during that period with parents looking for their sons, and if the missing boys weren't in my living room, chances were that Taz knew exactly where they were, who they were hanging out with, what movie they'd gone to see, or how to reach them by cell phone. "Your son is like the social director," one of the other parents commented. Indeed, he seemed happily woven in to a secure, safe, and friendly world.

Then they turned thirteen and got to eighth grade. Suddenly, Taz and all his friends were the biggest kids in the school. Many of them were taller than their teachers. They were jazzed about being "seniors" and going on to high school the next year. I could see there was a lot less time being spent on homework and a lot more time being spent on MySpace, cell phones, and iPods.

Taz's first-quarter grades in eighth grade were OK, but for the first time in middle school, he hadn't made the top ten student list. What was more troubling was that he didn't seem to care, and some of his friends had also dropped out of the top ten competition.

This was when they stopped hanging out at our house. For the first time in three years, I was coming home to an empty apartment. Taz's daily calls to check in by cell phone after school tapered off, too. When I tried to reach him, all I got was the familiar "Yo, whaddup! It's Taz!" but he wasn't returning my messages. I called the parents who used to ask Taz where their kids were, but they had no idea where Taz was.

One school night, it got to be nine o'clock and I hadn't heard from him. I left Sport with a neighbor and went out looking on the avenue near our house where I sometimes saw kids hanging out. I peered into the pizzeria, the Starbucks, and the shadowy playground where groups of teenagers often congregated. The kids who noticed me looked away quickly, guiltily putting their cigarettes behind their backs and stopping their loud stories midsentence, not knowing whose mother I was and whether they might be held accountable for whomever I was seeking. But I didn't recognize any of them, and Taz wasn't among them.

I walked from one end of the avenue to the other,

about a mile and a half round-trip, but didn't spot him anywhere. Then I walked up to the park where I sometimes, while walking the dog, saw teenagers gathering late at night to drink and smoke and do who knows what else. I had a whole speech prepared in my head about how dangerous it was for Taz to be in there this late, and how he should have called me, and how I didn't want him out on a school night, anyway. But I didn't get to make the speech. There was no teenage laughter coming from the park benches or the meadow where I'd seen kids in the past.

I sighed and headed home. I'm not the type to panic, but I wondered at what point was I supposed to call 911. I figured I'd try calling all his friends' parents again, as embarrassing as that would be, because it would just be more proof that I had no control over my son. And I'd try his cell again, too, before letting my worries get too extreme.

And then I guessed that I'd have no choice but to call the cops. "Oh, your thirteen-year-old is missing at ten p.m. on a Tuesday night? Trust me, lady, that's not an emergency," I could imagine the dispatcher laughing at me. But this had never happened before. To me, it was an emergency. In fact, the entire thirteenth year was starting to feel like one great big emergency.

I trudged up the steps to our building and opened the apartment door. There he was, grinning, standing with his dad and his brother, who'd been retrieved from the neighbor's house when Elon got home from work.

"Mom, where were you?" he said. "I tried to call you."

Indeed, the answering machine was blinking. I pressed Play.

"Hi, Mom, I'm at Trevor's house. Sorry I didn't call you before. I was hoping you could give me a ride, but I guess I'll take the bus. I'll be there around nine-thirty. See ya."

I felt like crying, but I wasn't sure why. I gave him a hug. "You have homework?"

"No."

I was sure he did. "Just go do it, quit fooling around," I said wearily. "I've been out looking for you for an hour, I'm exhausted. You should have called me a lot earlier than you did, and you never should have been out so late on a school night. You have no idea how upset I was."

He walked away. I told Elon how I'd been hunting for him up and down the avenue for an hour, how I went to the park in the dark imagining all kinds of terrible things had happened to him.

"You must have just missed his call," Elon said sympathetically.

Unfortunately, I didn't manage to miss the calls from Taz's school. The one about the soda can was among many complaints about his behavior in eighth grade, and I wasn't the only parent getting those types of calls from teachers. All of a sudden, now that they were the oldest kids in the school, kids who had been just fine in sixth and seventh grades were talking back to teachers, throwing things at each other, getting into fights, skipping classes, flunking tests, and missing homework all over the place.

It seemed like a day didn't go by when I didn't hear about an eighth grader getting into trouble. It was as if a switch had been flipped. The eleven- and twelve-year-olds who had draped themselves on my sofa had been replaced by evil proto-teenagers who were too cool to hang out in a living room under the watchful eye of a grown-up.

Not all the calls at my desk about Taz's obnoxious behavior were from school, however. One day Elon called to let me know that he gave Sport's keys to Taz that morning as the boys were heading out because Taz couldn't find his own keys.

I assured Elon that Taz's keys were on the floor of his room underneath a pile of dirty clothes, where they always are. I pointed out that now that Taz had Sport's keys, Sport would not be able to get into the house with his babysitter if he got home before Taz.

Elon had not considered this, but now it was too late.

At 3:15 p.m. that day, the phone at my desk rang. When you are a parent and the phone at your desk rings at 3:15 p.m., it is almost never good news. Indeed, it was the babysitter, calling from her cell phone, to say that Sport's keys were not in his bag, and Taz wasn't home, so they couldn't get inside our house.

I told her I would call Taz on his cell phone and tell him to go home to let them in.

I located Taz, who was hanging out with his friends in another neighborhood. He flat-out refused to head home to let Sport and the sitter in, and, to my utter astonishment, he then hung up.

My blood was boiling. I called Elon and quietly but urgently informed him that *he* had to call Taz and yell at him, as Elon has an office where he can shut the door, while I work in an enormous open newsroom surrounded by hundreds of other people, most of whom do not have obnoxious thirteen-year-olds and who would not understand why I was screaming my head off about why it's not OK to hang out with other people when your brother needs his keys back.

Elon called back a few moments later to say that everything was under control. Taz was en route home to let Sport in the house.

Then Taz called from his cell phone. He'd gotten home, but the key wasn't working. They couldn't get in the house.

I sighed and said I would be home as soon as I could. I silently thanked the God of Work for remote access that would enable me to finish my work from home and headed out. When I finally arrived, they were all sitting in the hallway, Sport, Taz, and the sitter, looking glum.

I tried my key, but just as with Sport's key, it didn't work.

"I have something to tell you, Mommy," Sport suddenly said in a small voice.

That is never a good sign, when they feel they have to

announce whatever it is they want to say with a formal introduction. What it really means is "I'm about to tell you something that is going to make you want to kill me."

I couldn't imagine what confession he felt the need to make at that particular moment. "What is it?" I said irritably.

He admitted that while he was waiting for Taz to come home with the key, he found a bobby pin on the floor of the hallway and shoved it in the door lock, thinking he could jimmy it open like they do in the movies.

But the bobby pin broke off. He opened his fist to show me the seven-eighths of the pin he was still holding. The little rubber tip was gone. Gone inside the lock. And that's why nobody's keys were working.

I paid the babysitter and sent her home. A lotta good she did me today. I could have yelled at her, and said, "OK, you were doing what exactly while Sport was sticking a bobby pin in the lock?" but there would just be no point. She was a teenager, too, a little older than Taz, and just about as useless.

There's a locksmith three blocks from our house. I ran down and caught the guy before he closed for the night. He dispatched someone to meet me at home, and I raced back.

The locksmith arrived, fidgeted with his tools and the lock for a few minutes, and, with a long, pincer-type thingie, he extracted the missing piece of the bobby pin from deep inside the lock mechanism.

I tried my key. It worked just fine.

The locksmith then handed me a bill for $93.

I asked the locksmith if he would like to adopt a child named Sport.

He politely declined.

"How about the other one," I said, pointing to Taz. "He's big enough that maybe you could put him to work. In fact, I'll pay you to take him."

Taz got a pained look on his face. "What did I do? I didn't put the bobby pin in the lock!"

"No, but if you hadn't lost your keys and taken Sport's this morning, this wouldn't have happened," I barked. "And furthermore, if you'd come right home when I first called you to let him in, instead of waiting until Dad yelled at you to do it, Sport might never have tried the bobby pin."

"That is so unfair!" he said.

The locksmith cleared his throat. "Cash, credit, or personal check," he said.

I sighed and got my checkbook, handed over the money, and started making dinner, a lovely rendition of frozen ravioli with sauce from a jar, with a healthy salad on the side that I assumed no one but me would touch. The entire time I made dinner, I was screaming my head off at my children.

At one point, Taz interrupted me to demand $25 of his bar mitzvah money to go buy a DVD.

The big bash had been a month earlier, and most of the money he'd received as gifts had gone into the bank.

I'd told him at the time that he would get a little bit of it as play money, but first he'd have to write thank-you notes.

"You don't get any money until the thank-you notes are done," I reminded him.

The DVD store closed at 7:30 p.m. It was then 6:10 p.m. He sat down with a pen and a stack of paper and wrote twenty thank-you notes in a half hour. He asked for the $25 again and promised to do the rest of the notes—another twenty or so—upon his return from the store. I demanded his cell phone as collateral. He agreed and handed it over.

The ravioli was done. I served dinner. I was still angry about the key, the lock, and the bill from the locksmith, so every three or four minutes or so, I would scream something at the top of my lungs like "You know, I work hard all day and I shouldn't have to come home to this nonsense!"

Sport, I felt, was responding appropriately, given his guilt. Basically, he wept quietly nonstop, and was looking suicidal. Unlike Taz, he apparently was still young enough that his conscience had not been obliterated by the hormones of puberty. He also refused to eat dinner.

Taz, on the other hand, ate a good portion of the ravioli, obviously untroubled by all that had transpired. Then he got up and headed to the DVD store, where he said he intended to buy a copy of *Terminator 2: Judgment Day*.

I walked down the hallway to his room. The sweater

he'd been wearing the day before was on the floor. I picked it up. His keys were underneath.

At times like that, I wish I were the type of person who could just go to a bar and order shots, and drink a whole line of them, and forget all my troubles. Unfortunately, I am not that kind of person; I am simply a Terrible Mother, and an all-too sober one at that.

Taz's behavior, unsurprisingly, both at home and at school, did not improve over the next few months. At some point, it got so bad that a Grand Inquisition was scheduled at school. I was ordered to appear at a meeting with two of his teachers, the guidance counselor, and the principal—all women. We sat at an oblong table in a classroom while they read the litany of offenses he'd committed. Most of them were on the order of bringing the soda can to class—minor in the scheme of things, but forming a pattern of disrespect. Moreover, his fall from the top ten to habitual troublemaker had been dramatic. Some kids had been bad since the day they'd arrived. Taz had been one of the good ones— until lately.

One of the examiners leaned toward him. "We're here because we're all very concerned about you," she said. "We don't understand what's going on."

Taz refused to make eye contact. But like any animal under attack, he puffed himself up as big as he could. He lifted his chin up to the ceiling, stretched one leg out to the side, and began bouncing the other knee up and down. He was wearing a sweatshirt so big it practically hung down to his knees. He stared at the ceiling, and shook his head. His backpack was in his lap and he put his arms across it.

"Well?" his inquisitor asked.

He shrugged and mumbled something like "ionhwanbehi," which we all instantly understood to mean "I don't want to be here."

"Is something going on? Are you having any problems? Because we're here to help," another one of the ladies said.

Around the table, manicured nails tapped on coffee cups, lipsticked lips were pursed, pantyhosed legs were crossed, pocketbooks were zipped open and closed. Yes, we were all there to help, but it was clear to me that no self-respecting thirteen-year-old boy would take help from this group of middle-aged females.

A long, uncomfortable minute ensued. Finally, he responded, shrugging again. "I just wanna get to high school."

There was nothing more to say or do. I went to work, he went to class. Later that day, I got a call from Mrs. L, who had been scheduled to attend the meeting but who hadn't been able to make it. She wanted to let me know that the other teachers had wanted to put a disciplinary letter in Taz's record, with a copy sent to the high school he was expecting to attend. If that happened, there was always a chance the high school could revoke his acceptance. Mrs. L said she'd argued against the disciplinary letter, and had prevailed—for now.

I thanked her for looking out for Taz. I told her I felt like she was some kind of guardian angel, and I thanked her for her call.

We hung up. I felt like crying.

Mrs. L was the same teacher who'd told me and Taz's father just a year and a half earlier at the parent-teacher conference that he was an extraordinary boy.

It seemed like that had been long time ago.

Back when he was eleven.

# THE EIGHTH-GRADE PROM

**E**ighth grade. Those two words have long been a code among friends from my own adolescence, because that was the year that we all acted out, drama queens and poseurs all, starring in our personal one-person plays about becoming teenagers.

There were the window-ledge sitters, the 3 a.m. phone callers, the ten-page letter writers, the spaced-out druggies, the stinking coughing smokers, the uncontrollable gigglers, the traumatized-by-dark-secrets mutes, the tough-girl authority challengers, the catatonic depression queens, the twitching overcaffeinated knee jigglers, the glittery eye-shadowed lip glossers, the obsessed-with-a-band fans, the long-haired bohemian poets, the grade grubbers, the porn readers, the guitar-playing hippies, the angry politicos, the in-your-face feminists, the sing-to-yourself weirdos, the change-the-world organizers, the pink-sweatered blow-dried preppies, and the sexy-dressed boy chasers.

On top of all of that, most of us were klutzy. We

called each other "spaz," for spastic. We spilled things, dropped things, broke things, lost things, and forgot things. We had bumps in places we didn't expect them, and arms and legs that seemed to elongate overnight; we accidentally smashed our heads on locker doors, our kneebones on desks, and our fingers in drawers. A few were too skinny, a few were too fat, and a few were still stuck in their little girlness, with white tights, ribboned pigtails, and patterned prim and pleated frocks. The rest had dandruff and pimples and BO and bad breath. We all needed tampons and bras, and the really bad girls needed birth control.

There were random victims who got inexplicably laughed about, picked on, and cruelly excluded; there were queen bees whose fingernail polish color choices were studied and whose sleepover guest lists were memorized and analyzed as carefully as the White House dinner seating chart for Queen Elizabeth's visit; and there were bullies who threatened and shook down and occasionally even hurt someone else. Some of us acted like we couldn't care less about anything: we were nihilists, existentialists, dreamers, and Buddhists. Others acted exactly the opposite: dramatic neurotics to whom everything mattered—every song lyric, every weather forecast, every headline, every calorie. Eighth grade was the year I learned the meaning of the words *histrionic* and *paranoid*, because they so often described the mental states of those around me.

And who was I? I wore leotards, hip-huggers, clogs, and

a smile; I wrote really bad poetry and played the guitar; and like a lot of kids I knew, I tried on all sorts of personas in pursuit of myself. I was bad, I was good; I was wacky and sane, moping one minute, silly the next. I talked too loudly or not loudly enough; I crouched and slithered and tried to be invisible when I couldn't bear the attention of those closest to me; or I stretched and sparkled and sang loudly in front of strangers. Sometimes I thought I was so smart I couldn't understand why the world hadn't noticed; other times I realized I'd been such an idiot that I fantasized about running away, changing my name and starting a new life in some exotic place like Minneapolis.

I got chicken pox in eighth grade and thought I'd rather die than go to class with all those marks on my face; I was worried everyone would think I had developed a terrible case of acne. Then I found out the French teacher thought I'd cut school all week in order to avoid a test. That raised my standing in the eyes of my peers. I wasn't pockmarked; I was delinquent! How cool. I figured it was worth returning, despite my disfigurement, to bask in my newfound status as a truant.

Even though I carry around all these memories of my own eighth grade inside me, for some reason they didn't help me when I was trying to make sense of my son's eighth-grade year. Maybe it was just too painful or embarrassing to admit that this had once been my reality, too.

I wonder sometimes if there's something to the old superstition about the number thirteen. Maybe that superstition was originally created by the mothers of some tribe who noticed that in their children's thirteenth year, they suddenly became possessed by evil spirits. Because it did seem that whenever Taz was around, things spilled and shattered, calm turned into chaos, and tempers were lost.

Noises came out of nowhere and material objects were inexplicably disturbed. Phones rang, music blared, alarms beeped, people were cursing, important papers tore, clothing was damaged, pictures fell off the walls.

Sometimes this spooky trail of destruction directly involved him, sometimes it involved his friends, and sometimes it seemed like pure physics. It was as if he were surrounded by a cloud of magnetic energy that caused lightning to strike, objects to tip over, and people to scream in his wake.

Perhaps it was the sudden bigness involved in turning thirteen; perhaps it's not being able to anticipate how much room you take up in a space that leads you to step on someone's toes or accidentally brush a glass from the counter to the floor as you pass by. Perhaps you become so obsessed with yourself that you can't think about those around you.

As a result, thank-yous and hellos go unsaid, and the general impression you leave among others is one of obnoxiousness. Or perhaps when you turn thirteen, you really, truly are possessed. I remember reading about teenage poltergeists and kinetic powers of adolescents, and I actually think I have experienced something like that living with a thirteen-year-old boy.

It was hard to remember sometimes that Taz had done well in school just a few months before. Once he turned thirteen, he just didn't care. Teachers who knew him from sixth and seventh grade were willing to cut him some slack, and he had a relationship with them, so if they said to him, "Hey, man, get with the program!" he would often straighten out.

But there were a number of new teachers who hadn't known him before. If he was being disrespectful, they were all too ready to write him off as a bad boy. After those blissful sixth- and seventh-grade reports, parent-teacher night had started to be painful again. Taz wouldn't listen, Taz wouldn't sit where he was supposed to, Taz was missing homework, Taz was hanging out with kids who smoked and cut class all the time, Taz was leaving the room without permission, Taz had told a teacher she was "retarded."

I was mortified at the description of the person they were telling me my son had become. I apologized to the teachers, and agreed with them that this was unacceptable behavior. I told them this wasn't how I had raised my son, but I'm not sure they believed me. At home, I yelled and screamed and even wept. I pleaded, cajoled, threatened, bribed, rewarded. But none of it did any good. The problem was, he wasn't listening. He had a look on his face that said, "I just don't care." I might as well have been talking to myself.

But I knew there was one big-ticket item that would get his attention. He desperately wanted a laptop for high school, and I wanted to get him one. There was a lot of competition in our house for use of the computer in the evenings, and most of Taz's teachers now routinely expected kids to use the Internet for research. Teachers wanted every paper typed, starting in sixth grade, and his father and I wanted to use the computer in the evenings, too, for e-mail and to catch up on things at work. Even his little brother liked using the computer to play games. A laptop for Taz would help ease the congestion.

So I told Taz I wanted to get him a laptop, but that I wouldn't if he kept getting in trouble at school. I was getting calls from teachers once a week, sometimes more than that. I needed him to improve his behavior at school, stop challenging the teachers over stupid things like whether he could have a soda in class, and get his homework done.

Where we live, there is no neighborhood public high school; you have to apply to high schools, just like college. Some of the schools have themes—they specialize in the arts or science, or they have a great sports program or are vocationally oriented. Taz had been accepted to a good school, with strong academics and a few bells and whistles like filmmaking classes and an interesting community service program. But with a couple more months of eighth grade to go, I had to remind Taz that it was not out of the question that this high school might revoke its acceptance if his middle school sent along a complaint. There was really a lot at stake, and not just the laptop.

But the way out was clear, I told him. Just cooperate, I begged, just do what they say. Just play by the rules. You don't have to love it, you just have to get through it.

Taz promised to change. We went a week, two weeks, then a month with no calls from school. I breathed a sigh of relief. Every time my phone rang at work and the caller ID showed a number that wasn't his school, I smiled.

Finally, we were literally down to one day left, graduation day, a Friday. I couldn't possibly get any calls that day—we were going to be at the school with him, for commencement in the auditorium. The day before, I'd even said to a colleague at work who enjoyed following my stories about Taz, "One day left and he graduates eighth grade! What could happen in one day?"

"You're home free!" my colleague agreed. "Congratulations."

The graduation was standard middle-school fare— blue nylon caps and gowns, a slide show, barely audible speeches from the valedictorian and salutatorian, cheers, songs, teachers crying, parents proud. Taz wasn't graduating with honors; his grades that year hadn't been good enough. But at least he was graduating. He'd gotten through it, and I planned to make good on my promise and get him the laptop over the weekend. His name was called, he went up on the stage, they handed him a diploma, and the deal was sealed.

The prom was that night. (This is another difference between being thirteen now and being thirteen a generation ago: now eighth graders have proms.) This was a ritual I had missed out on in my own teenage years. There was no prom at my all-girl school, so everything I knew about proms, I knew from TV and the movies. Limos? Tuxes? Corsages? I braced myself for all of that, even while thinking it would be absurd for middle school. But Taz said only the girls were getting dressed up, and he thought buying his date a bouquet was what was expected, not a corsage.

As for a limo, well, of course I was glad to hear they didn't need that, either. But I was a little puzzled about the transportation arrangements as Taz described them. We had gone to lunch, postgraduation, with a friend of Taz's and that boy's family, and I assumed the two kids would be going together to the prom that night, since they hung out a lot. This boy was one of Taz's longtime friends—one of the good ones.

But to my surprise, Taz revealed that he and this boy were not traveling to the prom together.

Taz then explained that he planned to meet his prom date in the neighborhood where she lived, and then they'd meet up with some other kids near there, and travel as a group to the dance, which was being held in a catering hall that the PTA had rented for the occasion.

Throughout my years as a mother, I have occasionally been seized with moments of extraordinary foreboding. It's a sixth sense that I think all mothers have at some level. There are times when you just get this terrible feeling that something bad is going to happen. You don't know what it is, but your whole body is suddenly cramped with cold. The hair on the back of your neck literally stands up. It's positively primeval. You have morphed into one giant instinct, but you can't quite connect well enough with your primordial self to know what it's trying to tell you. Your brain starts to shuffle scenarios, looking to fill in the blank after the question mark. But you can't quite put your finger on what's wrong.

There was something about the scenario Taz was describing about traveling to the prom that made me uncomfortable. But I just couldn't pinpoint the gap. Something bad was going to happen, I just knew it. I could feel it. But there was also an inevitability about it. It didn't seem like there was anything I could do to avert whatever was going to happen.

Not that I didn't try. We went home after lunch in the restaurant. Taz was supposed to pick up his date later in the day. I didn't know her, but I'd heard her name, and the names of some of the kids they were planning to meet, from other teachers. None of them were among the good kids he'd spent most of sixth and seventh grade with. These were kids the other teachers had warned me about—kids they'd said were bringing each other down, kids who smoked and cut class and got bad grades. I should have paid more attention to the prom plans all along, but now they were set, and I didn't see any way of changing them. All I could do was lecture. And so I did.

"Taz," I said, trying not to sound too desperate, "I have a bad feeling about tonight. I just have this feeling something bad is going to happen. Please don't let these kids get you into trouble. If someone is doing something they shouldn't do, walk away. Don't let other people bring you down. You know that adults will judge you based on the company you keep. Don't let anyone judge you tonight because of something someone else is doing."

He nodded as if he'd heard me, but I wasn't sure he had.

He was dressed, like most of the boys going to the party, very informally—a T-shirt and baggy pants. Aside from the hundred-dollar Jordans, which by now were de rigueur in his wardrobe, his hat was about the most stylish and significant component of his wardrobe. It was a Yankees cap, but covered with elaborate patterned stitching. It was crisp and clean, and he wore it as proudly as Fred Astaire in a top hat.

It had turned into a hot, humid early summer day. Our old car has no air-conditioning, so we drove to his date's house with the windows rolled down. I had offered to drive him and the others in their group to the party, but he said they'd rather take a car service. And I could see how our beat-up car, with no radio and no AC, wasn't exactly fit to take Cinderella to the ball.

We arrived at his date's house and he knocked on the

door. She emerged like a dream. She really, truly looked beautiful, like a princess in a storybook. She was wearing such a pretty dress. It didn't look expensive, but it was just perfect. Pale pink, satiny, with a fitted bodice and a long poufy skirt. As she and Taz posed for pictures, it was all a bit surreal. She was so dressed up, holding the flowers Taz had bought for her, and Taz was so casual about the whole thing.

The girl lived with her mother in an old house on a quiet corner of an industrial neighborhood; she and Taz posed for pictures in front of a little overgrown garden. I immediately connected with the mom, who had long gray braids and appeared to be about my age. She was a hippie type, and it was clear that she loved this girl with all her heart, and was trying hard to raise her right.

But somehow the picture just didn't quite add up. This lovely girl, all dressed up in front of this run-down house, posing for pictures with a boy in a baseball cap. Again I was hit with that wave of foreboding, like a shiver running through me from head to toe. I just couldn't shake the worry that something bad was going to happen.

The kids were about to get into the car so I could drop them off a mile or so away, where they were meeting the others in their group, when I suddenly put my arms around the girl and her mom and pulled them in close to me. I called Taz over to join our little séance.

"Listen," I said, "I just want to say one thing. I want you two to have a great time tonight, and I know you will. But I just want to be sure you understand that you have to behave yourselves and follow all the rules. I said this to Taz before we left our house, and I'm just going to say it again here now. Sometimes bad things happen at these kinds of events. And you guys have to look out for each other. You have to walk away, and help each other walk away, if someone else is doing something bad. Don't let other people drag you down!"

There was a quiver in my voice and the girl's mother looked at me. Our eyes met, and I could see she understood. A moment ago, we'd both been smiling at how lovely her daughter looked. But now the happy look was gone. That same wave of foreboding, I could tell, was passing through her, too. She added her voice to mine.

"Listen to what Taz's mom is saying," she urged. "She's absolutely right. You two need to make sure you don't get into any trouble tonight."

We bade our good-byes and left. It was hot in the car and we were all sweating; the breeze gusting in through the open windows didn't help. I worried that Taz's date's dress was going to be ruined in the heat, and I thought to myself it was just as well they were taking a nice air-conditioned cab to the party. Taz called his friends on his cell phone to say we were on our way, and a few minutes later I dropped them off. I saw a small cluster of kids—the girls all dressed up like Taz's date in long, pretty dresses, the boys all wearing T-shirts, baggy jeans, fancy shoes, and baseball caps.

"Yo!" I heard one of them call as Taz and the girl left the car.

I tossed Taz a $20 bill to help pay for the taxi, since the catering hall was a good half hour away. I reminded him to call me if he or anyone else needed a ride home.

As he walked away, I got the shiver again.

"Taz," I called out. He swiveled his face around to half look at me, clearly annoyed that I had called him back into my world just as he was crossing over into his.

"Do the right thing," I said. "OK?"

He nodded and walked off.

I drove home and changed into my grungiest tank top and cutoff shorts. My younger son was playing with a neighbor's child, Elon was working late at the office, and I was going to give the house a good, thorough cleaning. I started loading the washer in the basement with bedspreads, curtains, and towels; I put Bruce Springsteen loud on the CD player and got out the vacuum cleaner. I scrubbed the tub and dusted. It was hot in the apartment, and with all this hard work, I was getting sweaty and grimy. No matter; I'd soon be done, take a shower, and then get to enjoy my nice clean house all weekend.

I almost didn't hear the phone over the noise of the vacuum cleaner and the music. It had to ring two or three times before I picked the sound out. I flipped the vacuum off with my foot, dropped the hose, and caught the call on what was probably the fourth ring, right before the answering machine kicked in.

"Hello," I panted.

"Is this Taz's mother?"

My heart sank. Something had happened. I knew it!

"Yes," I said in a small voice.

Inside my head, a taunt was building: "Terrible Mother, Terrible Mother, TERRIBLE MOTHER!"

"This is the guidance counselor. You need to come right away and pick Taz up. We had to kick him and a few other kids out of the prom because they tried to bring in alcohol."

I sighed and very nearly let out a sob. I asked for the address and said I would be there as soon as I could. I went over to the neighbor's house where Sport was playing and told him he had to come right away. "Your brother's in a lot of trouble and we have to go get him," I said.

I parked around the corner from the catering hall. I slammed the car door, grabbed Sport's hand, and half dragged him as I marched down the block. Sorrow had given way to fury. Right then I felt like killing Taz with my bare hands in front of the world. I was also conscious of the fact that my face was streaked with dirt, my hair was a mess, my unshaven legs were on display beneath my dirty cutoff jeans and sweaty tank top. I looked like a crazy person, and I felt like one, too.

The party hall was one of those faux elegant places with the front steps covered in red carpeting beneath a white canopy. A few moms from the PTA were standing outside smoking or making calls on their cells. They were all dressed up, their hair coiffed to perfection, jewelry, nails, shoes matching their pocketbooks, and all of that.

I came pounding up the red carpet, my flip-flops slapping each step, my younger son almost in tears himself from the stress of it all, but too scared by my mood to utter a word. On top of everything else, I now had to imagine the chatter about myself: "And you should have seen the mother—what a mess! No wonder the kid's out of control."

Just before I flung open the gold-embossed glass door to pull Taz out, I spotted his date. She was standing outside, I guess waiting to be picked up by her mother. Funny thing was, she didn't look at all upset. She still looked beautiful, dewy, like Cinderella must have been around ten o'clock the night of the ball, with hours to go before her coach would arrive. She even gave me a sweet little smile.

I was having none of it. At that moment, I hated her just as much as I hated Taz. I wanted to smack her, but restrained myself.

"You should be ashamed of yourself," I screamed, getting right up in her face before flip-flopping away. She recoiled in horror, as if the evil stepmother herself had broken the spell, and the other mothers looked up from their cigarettes and cell phones for a moment, trying to figure out what was going on.

But I didn't stay in their view long enough. I stepped over the threshold and saw Taz sitting in the lobby with another mother. A wonderful, sweet, and smart mother whom I admired tremendously. Her son was one of the nicest, smartest boys in the school. The boy's father had died when he was young, and his mother was not only doing a great job raising her kids, but she also had a job and volunteered a tremendous amount of time to the school. And here she was, giving comfort to My Evil Son, like a Saint Among the Lepers.

Taz saw me the instant my head poked through the door, abruptly rose, and walked toward me. At the same time, I spotted the guidance counselor who'd called me to come get him. I nodded at her, making sure that she saw I was picking him up. I didn't want to have to speak to her or anyone else there. I stormed back down the red carpet, past Taz's date, past the moms on their cell phones, still holding Sport by the hand, with Taz following. We got around the corner and a third of the way down the block to near where I'd parked the car when I stopped and let him have it, at the top of my lungs, right there on the street.

"I knew something bad was going to happen! I knew it! I begged you to do the right thing, I told you to behave yourself, and you had to go break the rules! What is wrong with you? How could you do this? Do you know how embarrassing this is, not just for me but for your whole family? From the time you were born I've given you nothing but love, and this is the thanks I get—you get kicked out of your prom! There is no excuse for you, Taz! Other kids have a tough life and they turn out just fine, but you, you've had everything you ever wanted and all you can do is screw up! I am so ashamed of you, and I hope you have the decency to be ashamed of yourself!"

Taz looked like he was about to cry. He hung his head beneath his baseball cap and shuffled along in his perfect white Jordans. I realized a half-dozen people up and down the block had stopped in their tracks to stare at us, trying to figure out what was going on. Suddenly, I had visions of someone calling 911 to report child abuse. Two guys in their late twenties standing directly across the street from us had paused their conversation to stare and watch the show.

"What's the matter with you?" I screamed at them. "Weren't you ever a teenager? Didn't you ever make your mother so mad that she started yelling at you in the street? Mind your own business!"

They looked at each other, somewhat terrified, and resumed walking without saying a word back. I realized at that moment that I had crossed over from being a Terrible Mother to being a Lunatic Mother. It was not a pleasant thought. I unlocked the car door in a hurry and got in.

I can't remember exactly what I said on the ride home, or that night, or that weekend. All I know is that I basically repeated, sometimes screaming, sometimes crying, sometimes whispering, the rant I'd started as we left the hall. I dreaded the call I was going to have to make to Elon, who, upon hearing what had happened, reacted the way he often did—by saying nothing. He had an even dimmer view of Taz's shenanigans than I did, so that whereas I was always shocked, horrified, and disappointed to learn about Taz's latest escapades, Elon usually reacted with something closer to grim resignation, as if he'd known it was going to end this way all along. It was as if the crisis du jour was nothing more than an affirmation of his previously held opinions that we were heading to a very, very bad place.

I tried to get the whole story of what had happened from Taz, from the guidance counselor, and from some of the other kids who'd been there. But I never did piece it together entirely. The best I could figure was that after I dropped Taz and his date off, instead of calling a taxi to go to the prom, the group went to a park to hang out for a while.

At some point, someone purchased a flask of Bacardi with the intent of bringing it to the prom. They arrived late, after most of the other kids had gone in, and realized that bouncers were searching everyone heading into the hall. They turned tail and walked back outside, not realizing they were being followed by one of the bouncers, who then told a school official that he had seen Taz tossing the flask of Bacardi into the bushes outside the hall.

The bouncer had retrieved the bottle as evidence, and all the kids in the group had been grabbed before they could go inside.

Taz, of course, claimed some level of innocence. He said he had neither bought nor carried in nor dumped the bottle in the bushes, although he admitted being part of the offending group. I insisted that it didn't matter, that the incident had borne out exactly what I had tried to tell him that day—that he would be judged by the company he kept.

"Grown-ups don't care whether you did the crime or were just hanging out with people who did the crime," I explained calmly in one of my more rational moments. "You're guilty, either way."

For his part, Taz spent the weekend padding quietly around the house, keeping as low a profile as possible. In response to my periodic outbursts, he assumed the stance of a Japanese penitent, head bowed, nodding, eyes down, mumbling, "I'm sorry. I'll change. I promise. I'll make new friends. I've learned from my mistakes. I understand what I did was wrong. You were right. I was stupid. I'm sorry. I'll change. I promise . . ."

The mother of a friend of Sport's called the next day to arrange a playdate, and when she asked how I was, I simply burst into tears and mumbled something like "Be glad your kid is only eight!" I finally retreated to my bed with a basket of mending that had been piling up for months. I don't like sewing, and I'm not very good at it, despite growing up with a mother who could cut her own patterns and sew anything from a bathing suit to a coat. So when something rips or needs to be altered or hemmed, I just throw it in a pile on an old sewing box filled with pins and needles, a dozen spools of thread in various colors and textures, and things that I almost never use, like pinking shears.

That afternoon, I sat with a dozen items that had accumulated over a course of months and I sewed every last one of them. I hemmed, I mended, I altered. It was about the most calming thing I could have done—a repetitive, meticulous task that kept me focused and productive. It occurred to me that maybe the reason people have to take so much antianxiety medication and go to spas and take yoga classes to calm down is that they've given up sewing. By the time the last pair of pants was done, I felt almost normal.

At one point during my sewing–mental health session, the phone rang. It was Taz's date's mom. She was calling to ask me if I had any information about what had happened. I told her what I knew, which wasn't much more than what she knew, and I told her I felt really, really bad about having walked up to her daughter outside the party hall and screamed at her. To my surprise, she said she was glad I'd done it. She told me that a couple of the kids—her daughter included—had taken off, just disappeared before their parents and guardians had arrived to take them home.

"They were planning to party, and they weren't going to let anything get in their way, so they stayed out all night, and came home this morning," she said. She sounded angry. I could only imagine how frantic I would have been had Taz gone that route. Thank God he was there when I got there! What if he'd taken off? I would have called the cops and reported him missing; I would have thought he was dead.

That night, Saturday night, Taz had planned to have a few of his old friends over—his good friends, not the kids he'd gone to the prom with—for pizza and to watch a video. I considered making him cancel the party but in the end decided to let the kids come over. They were kids I wanted him to continue to be friends with, and I worried that turning them away on the last weekend of the school year might make it harder for them to stay in touch over the summer. None of the bad kids from the prom had been on the guest list for this little gathering; these were the four or five kids he'd been friends with since sixth grade, the ones he used to vie with for top grades and awards.

As they sat around our living room that evening playing a video game, Taz's father decided to undertake an investigation of his own, *Law & Order* style. Taz's father is a criminal appeals lawyer; all of his clients are already in jail by the time he gets their cases, so he often deals with people who have already been convicted, but who are trying desperately to prove their innocence.

To his credit, Taz's father had not been nearly as hysterical as I had been about this whole incident, but that was mainly due to the fact that his expectations were so low to begin with. Now he strode into the living room, approached the sofa where the boys were draped, holding controllers and watching the aliens of Halo destroy each other, and cleared his throat.

The boys looked up. One of them let out a chuckle and, realizing what was about to unfold, mumbled something like "This is going to be good."

"So, Taz," Elon began.

Taz looked up and grinned, seeing in his father a worthy adversary for the game that was about to unfold. "Yes?" he responded cheekily.

"So you say that you are basically innocent regarding what happened last night."

"Yes."

"I see." He folded his arms and took three steps, then put up a finger before asking his next question. It was just like on TV, and it was kind of fun and thrilling to watch.

I took a seat in the mushy armchair, called the dog over to pat while I watched, and made myself comfy for the show.

"Let me ask you something," Elon said. "What type of alcohol was it that the bouncer found in the bushes?"

"It wasn't me!" Taz insisted.

"I didn't say it was you. I just asked you what type of alcohol it was."

"Bacardi. You know that. They told Mom."

"What kind of Bacardi?"

"I don't know! I think—probably apple."

"About how much does that go for?"

He shrugged and eyed his friends. "I think about seven dollars."

"And how would you know that?"

"Dad, I didn't buy it!"

"I didn't say you bought it. I asked you how you would know how much it costs if you didn't buy it and you had nothing to do with it."

One of his friends gave Taz a look and said, "You might as well tell them what really happened. What they're thinking is worse than the truth, yo."

Elon paused for a minute and looked at me. Was that line from Taz's friend a setup—"What they're thinking is worse than the truth"—intended to throw us off the trail here? Or were we really thinking that Taz was more involved than he actually was in this whole incident?

Elon and Taz continued sparring for a few more rounds, but no more information was revealed than what we already had. I still to this day occasionally ask Taz what happened, but he refuses to tell the whole story—whether out of loyalty to the other kids or to cover his own butt, I'll never know.

That Monday there was no school, but the eighth graders were actually supposed to come back in for one more day, Tuesday, to pick up their report cards and say one last good-bye to their friends, teachers, and to middle school before taking off for high school. I was at work that Monday and Taz was at home when the phone rang at my desk. Incredibly, when I looked at the caller ID, I realized it was the school. Not again! What could they possibly want to tell me now?

It was the guidance counselor, calling to tell me that the principal had decided that Taz couldn't come in to pick up his report card the next day because of what happened at the prom. I asked to speak to the principal, but the guidance counselor said she wasn't available.

I felt heartbroken for Taz. True, he had been a very

bad boy. He had broken a rule that no thirteen-year-old should ever break. His grades had plummeted. He'd gone from being a star student to being a problem. Was it just his age, or was he really on a downward spiral? I knew he would be very upset that he was being banned from saying good-bye to the place he had spent the last three years.

I decided to dig in my heels for once and try to bail him out. I told the guidance counselor that I didn't think it was fair to keep him away the last day, and I took a deep breath to make a little speech that had suddenly popped into my head.

"He's already been punished," I said. "You kicked him out of the prom before he even got in. We paid for him to go, and he never got to enjoy any part of it. I'm not saying he's innocent, but, on the other hand, none of us actually knows for sure what he did. All you have is a bouncer saying he thinks it was Taz who did something as part of a larger group. There's no evidence. It didn't happen during the school day. It was a PTA event, and I really don't see legally how you have the right to bar him from school for something you can't even be certain he did, when it wasn't even on school property."

The guidance counselor didn't say anything for a moment. She was one of the people at school that had known Taz for a while and who liked Taz. I don't think she truly thought of him as a bad boy.

Finally, she told me to write a letter and fax it in. She

said she'd show it to her higher-ups, and see what they said.

I hastily typed up a note, summing up what I'd said to her on the phone, and adding a little drama. "Is there no redemption in this world?" I wrote. "It does not seem right to deprive him of the chance to say good-bye to his teachers after three years."

A few minutes later, the phone rang. It was the last call I'd ever get from that school, and it was a reprieve. Taz could come in the next day, get his report card, and say good-bye.

And so he did. His report card wasn't totally abysmal—he'd somehow managed to squeak out a B average. And he had a question for me when I got home.

"Can we go get that laptop now?"

The answer, needless to say, was no.

# CONTRABAND

**W**e sent Taz away for a few weeks when the horror year known as eighth grade was finally over and summer began. And while he was gone, I decided to undertake a major archaeological excavation. In other words, cleaning his room, one layer at a time. I started with the piles on the floor, the way I imagine geologists peel back soil and stone in search of fossils.

The top layer was easy. Dirty clothes. Under that, evidence that whatever lived in this room was sustained by a diet of Gatorade and Twizzlers. Next, school train passes that expired a year ago, an ancient *Us* magazine announcing Brangelina's pregnancy, and a couple of empty cans of Axe. A few layers down, when I found homework from third grade, I knew I had almost reached the molten Inner Core.

Ah, but what was this under the bed, with the fuzzy balls of dog hair, the stray sock, the moldy towel, and the Orbit gum wrappers? I appeared to have found the secret treasure. A lockbox, where the inhabitant of this world had no doubt hidden his most prized possessions. Like any good archaeologist, or should I say like any mother, I was extremely curious to know what was in there.

I wondered innocently where the key might be. Not that I was hunting for it, but didn't I see it over by the expired train passes? Hmm, perhaps that was it. I decided it wouldn't hurt to just take a quick look and see what a thirteen-year-old considers worth keeping under lock and key. Chances were there was nothing in there but a $2 bill and a Kennedy half-dollar. Don't all kids love to hide money? I figured I'd just take a peek, then lock it up and put the key away, and he'd never have to know.

OH MY GOD. This was far worse than anything I ever imagined. Two water bottles filled with what smelled like bourbon! (Only a thirteen-year-old would put brown alcohol in a water bottle, when vodka or gin might have gone unnoticed.) And what was in this bag, wrapped up in a tissue, inside another bag, wrapped up in tin foil? Some kind of . . . herb? Drug? Tea?

This was so embarrassing. I was born in the sixties and I'm not sure what pot looks like! It's just that, well, I was never much of a smoker. I reminded myself that the term of art now is weed, not pot, in case I had to discuss this with Taz or anyone else under the age of thirty, and I continued my investigation. The most troubling part was yet to come. There were, like, condoms in here! Not one or two, but a dozen! Where did he get them? Why does he have them? When did my thirteen-year-old decide he needed to be prepared for safe sex? And was that a good thing or a bad thing?

Worst of all, now that I'd found all this stuff in the lockbox, I had no idea what to do with it. Should I confiscate it? Put it back and pretend I never found it? Check again in a few months to see if he'd progressed to manufacturing crystal meth? Make an appointment with a psychiatrist or save myself $800 and just turn my entire family in to the Drug Enforcement Administration? Or maybe don't bother with the feds. Go local, to Child Welfare. No, I decided, that's no good. They'd probably send Taz and Sport to live with wacko foster parents who'd starve and beat them while partying on their monthly checks.

I reminded myself that I Am a Terrible Mother. But I tried to look on the bright side. At least there was no porn in the box. Then I realized that was probably hidden on our computer somewhere. And if I were to find porn there, I'd already decided I would try to follow the example of a friend from abroad. When she found her son with a picture of a woman with her boobs hanging out, she simply said, "I'm European. You can't shock me." And walked away. So I had been practicing saying aloud, "I'm American. You can't shock me!"

Then I looked up at the posters Taz had hanging on his bedroom walls. The Olsen twins were up there, along with Angelina. A couple of basketball stars, and the ad for *The School of Rock*. It all seemed so innocent, and sweet. But then I noticed Eminem. And the poster for *Hustle & Flow*. This room's rating went from PG to R some time ago, and I obviously wasn't paying attention.

Did I mention, by the way, where Taz was as I stood in his room looking at the walls, cleaning out the garbage and discovering all that stuff I wished I hadn't discovered?

He was in Australia.

Yes, Australia. A place I have never been, and probably never will go because I can't afford it. Don't ask me how I was able to send my son there. It has something to do with the fact that sleepaway camp in New Jersey costs $1,500 a week, so it made a teen trip to the other side of the world look inexpensive. OK, so I raided my retirement fund to help pay for it. It was worth the peace and quiet I had in the few hours I managed to be at home each day that summer without engaging in screaming fights with Taz. After all those calls from school, after the prom night debacle, I was just as happy to have him out of my hair, out of my time zone, and out of my hemisphere for a while that summer, and he was just as happy to leave.

Still, the fact that the only person I personally know who has been to Australia is my thirteen-year-old son is truly mind-boggling. All the adults I know can barely afford to drive to the Jersey shore for a week in July. I sincerely hope that there is reincarnation, so that in my next life, I can come back as a thirteen-year-old, because thirteen-year-olds these days live a life that no grown-up can ever hope to live.

Taz had gone to Australia with a youth organization that takes kids around the world. There were kids profiled in the promotional brochure for this organization that are, like, sixteen years old and they've already been to every continent on the planet, including Antarctica (not to mention already having been vaccinated against every disease on the face of the earth except maybe rabies. And I actually think for some countries, they recommend that, too, as protection from mad dogs.).

In some ways, though, it was better than sending him to summer camp in, for example, Pennsylvania, because he was so far away, he couldn't ask for any more money than we had already spent to send him there. The time difference was so bizarre that he couldn't figure out when to call us. It was always fourteen hours ago tomorrow when he tried to use his phone card to reach us, and we were never home.

Later, we'd find strange messages on the answering machine at 8 p.m. saying things like, "Oh, hi . . . it's six-thirty in the morning here and I just woke up and we're heading out to throw boomerangs in the koala preserve . . . I need to ask you something but I guess I'll try to call back." If he had been in camp near home, he might have been able to get hold of one of us and demand that we deliver candy or cash or who knows what else before sundown.

So that was part of why we didn't feel sad or worried

putting him on the plane. But he also had no qualms about taking this trip without us, and I'd been impressed that he was so curious about a place most Americans know almost nothing about.

When he was eleven, he went to camp in Kansas with a friend, and I cried for two days after he got on the plane. I wasn't sure he could handle the ups and downs of travel without me, and, as it turned out, he'd ended up on the flight from hell—delays, cancellations, sitting on the tarmac for hours, waiting out a storm. He was supposed to arrive in Kansas at 3 p.m. and he didn't get there until 3 a.m. That was partly why I'd felt so sad about it, because I wasn't there with him when he had to endure all those problems. Of course, he had a great time in Kansas, anyway—despite the fact that he had left all of his socks home and had to wear the same pair the whole week.

But when we sent him to Australia, I knew he was mature enough and savvy enough that he'd be just fine whether facing a plane delay, jet lag, bad weather, an unpleasant roommate, icky food, getting lost, or just the lack of clean socks. (One of the good things about boys is, they're OK with dirt. Really.) Besides, I needed a break from all his shenanigans.

So seeing him off at the airport, once he checked in with his group and we'd made sure for the thousandth time that he had his passport, his ticket, his wallet, his iPod, and everything else he needed for the twenty-four-hour plane ride, just wasn't that emotional. Elon and I bade our good-byes and tried not to embarrass him in front of the other kids as we hugged him and wished him well. Then we walked out of the terminal and got on the bus to the parking lot.

There we encountered one of the other mothers from the group. I saw that behind her hastily donned sunglasses, her eyes were flooded with tears. I gave her a hug and assured her the kids would be fine, that this was an experience they'd remember forever.

"Now stop crying," I said to her, "because you're going to make me cry."

But that was a lie. I didn't feel like crying in the slightest. I could only feel relieved. It was sort of like what a friend told me when she finally sent her son off to college. The kid had been acting like such a jerk that saying good-bye proved far easier than she ever imagined.

Of course, the other aspect of Taz being in Australia was that I couldn't exactly call him up and say, "What the hell is going on with all this stuff I found in your room?" That conversation would have to wait until he got home, which would give me plenty of time to figure out the right way to handle it all.

I decided to ask a couple of friends whose kids were going off to college in September how they'd dealt with these situations. "So," I e-mailed one of them, "what would you do if you found contraband in your son's room?"

"What sort of contraband?" he cheerfully responded. "Would that be pornography? Weapons? Narcotics?"

His flippant tone suggested that he couldn't imagine what I was dealing with. I couldn't bear to admit the whole truth, so I only told him about the alcohol. He responded that he'd never had a problem like that, despite being the father of teenagers. Once, he added, some cash was missing from the household, and he told the kids that if it were returned, there would be no questions asked. The money was back by nightfall.

OK, so Mr. Goody Two Shoes and his Perfect Family were not going to be much help. I e-mailed someone else, this time someone who likes to party. He also has a couple of kids older than mine. Well, he said, once when his daughter was sixteen, she came home really drunk, and they took her cell phone away for a week, but that was about it.

Thanks anyway, but that wasn't much help, either. Taz accidentally dropped his cell phone in the toilet a month before I found the lockbox, and I'd done nothing to replace it, so I couldn't punish him by taking away something that didn't work. Besides, if he were sixteen instead of thirteen, this wouldn't have been so bad.

I asked my sister if she had any advice, but she laughed at the notion that anyone would come to her for advice on raising teenagers. "I don't know," she said. "I failed that part of being a mommy." Even though she claims she failed, her daughter grew up to be a lovely young woman, gainfully employed as a nurse, the type of girl any parent would be proud of. I wondered if some day when Taz was grown up, people would also have a hard time believing that he put us through the wringer when he was a kid.

I thought about consulting some of the mommies in our neighborhood, but I quickly abandoned the idea. You see, most of these mommies are Perfect Mommies, and I am not. In fact, I have long lived in fear of their judgment. I've never been able to compete on their level or meet their standards, and so I don't even try. I refer to myself as one of the IPM, the Imperfect Mommies, but we are a despicable minority in the nabe, easily recognized by our unkempt hair, our lack of enthusiasm for PTA events and soccer games, and our failure to insist that all taxis come equipped with car seats and that every child be slathered in SPF 30 sunscreen every day from April to September.

Now, the differences between the PMs and the IPMs actually started to become clear to me very early on, when I was pregnant. The other pregnant mommies were all buying elegant dresses at a store called Pea in the Pod, but I was too cheap to go out and spend money on nice maternity clothes and shoes that actually fit my swollen feet, so I just wore down the backs of my shoes until my heels hung over the edge, and bought some skirts with elastic waistbands and smocklike jersey tops at Kmart. I remember this one skirt in particular that was lavender, and I had found a matching top to go with it, which pleased me to no end. I had never been a purple person before, but somehow being enormously pregnant seemed like the perfect opportunity to experiment with a new wardrobe palette.

Given my sartorial state, I shouldn't have been surprised when a woman I knew took pity on me after her daughter was born and loaned me three beautiful maternity dresses that she no longer needed. I wore them every Tuesday, Wednesday, and Thursday for the last three months of my pregnancy. (Monday and Friday I wore the Kmart outfits and hoped no one would comment on the contrast.) After I gave birth, I had the dresses dry-cleaned and returned them to her. But she didn't feel the need to have a second child, so she didn't want the clothes back.

That was OK; they came in handy when I got pregnant the second time. See, unlike my benefactress, I knew I'd need another child if only to prove that nature, not nurture, was the explanation for all my problems as a parent.

The PMs tormented me after the baby was born, too. They would sometimes call me at night on the phone, after I had gone back to work, kind of like how the popular girl in high school who wasn't really my friend would sometimes call me to get the math homework but would never call me to invite me to her sleepovers. I always knew I was in trouble when a PM began the conversation with statements like "I almost didn't call you . . . I wasn't sure you'd want to know this but . . . I saw your babysitter today at the playground . . . and . . ."

And what? In that excruciating moment before she got around to actually describing what she had seen, the most horrifying forms of abuse would occur to me. Perhaps the PM had seen my baby crying hysterically, strapped into his stroller, while my babysitter chatted with her friend! (I'd seen that plenty of times myself, but could never bring myself to tell the unsuspecting mothers, even though I sometimes knew them well.) Or maybe the PM had seen the sitter feeding my baby McDonald's french fries, or offering a sip from her own diet soda filled with chemicals! Digging even deeper into the abyss of the pit of tortures no yuppie mother wants to hear that her baby has endured at the hands of a sitter was corporal punishment. Please don't tell me you saw my sitter hit my baby! I actually didn't think it was possible that a report like that would get back to me by phone in the evening. Surely any PM worth her latte would whip out a cell phone and call the cops on the spot if she ever saw a babysitter smack a child in our rarefied little corner of the playground.

But no, as it turned out, none of these things were what had impelled one of these caring woman to reluctantly phone me one night. Instead, the revelation that ensued was not about abuse so much as what she considered to be neglect. My irresponsible babysitter had allowed little Taz to go barefoot in the sandbox. A discussion followed about all of the harmful things that might be in the sandbox. Like broken glass or pigeon poop. Or squirrel poop or doggie poop. Then a discussion ensued about what exactly my babysitter looked like, because she was fairly sure it was my sitter ("She has dark hair, right?") and Taz ("He's blonde, right?"), but she couldn't be 100 percent sure. She did note that in her opinion, my sitter was quite good-looking, and she somehow made this seem like it was my fault, too. (Maybe I was trying to wreck my marriage in addition to harming my child?) But actually my sitter, while not unattractive, was, in my opinion, a rather unremarkable-looking middle-aged woman, and I said so.

"Oh no," my informant insisted. "She's very voluptuous!"

This was getting weird. And then a discussion ensued about whether I actually considered the sandbox accusation a fireable offense, and when it became clear that I didn't, well, I suppose that only underscored the inadequacies that led me to have such an irresponsible babysitter in the first place. The phone call was finally, mercifully, over.

As Taz grew older and Sport was born, the PMs never left my life; they just moved onto other things. Did I know Taz had sneaked out of afterschool in third grade to go to the candy store? Well, no, I didn't know that, because of course the reason he was in afterschool was so that I could work. Did I know he was Rollerblading without his wrist guards? Running in the street after a ball? Biking without a helmet? Yeah yeah yeah, he'd been on the road to hell since he went in that sandbox barefoot. And what had I been doing about it? Nothing! Why? Because I'm an IPM, not a PM.

There weren't quite as many reports from the PMs

regarding Sport, but the few that did come in were memorable. He's a very agile child, with a sensibility sort of like a mountain goat, and when he was in kindergarten, he figured out how to climb up to the tippy top of a piece of equipment on the school playground that was not designed to be climbed on but was actually ornamental. It was like a small cupola high above a domed climbing apparatus, and he loved to scramble up and perch there like an owl, looking down on the rest of us from twenty feet above.

I'd cower in a corner of the schoolyard whenever he did this, pretending not to notice and hoping that the PMs didn't realize he was my child. But then one day I heard a passerby on the street call up to him, "Hey little boy, where's your mother?" My cover was blown; I had to fess up.

"I'm right here," I croaked, and waved, then shrugged in response to the stranger's quizzical stare. "It's not easy being Spider-Man's mother, ha-ha-ha," I added with a feeble laugh, but the Righteous Citizen did not appear amused.

I stood beneath the jungle gym and pleaded urgently with Sport to come down before somebody called the cops. Eventually, he did, proving that unlike his older brother, he at least cares what the rest of the world thinks, or cares enough about what I think the rest of the world thinks to help me out.

Actually, for a while there, I aspired to be a PM. But in the end, I realized that it takes not just wisdom and problem solving to be a PM; it also takes a certain amount of competitiveness, and I've never been good at that sort of thing. I prefer to be in my own little world, cluelessly casting about for perfection than measuring myself against others. I just don't care if I have round-toed shoes when everyone else has pointy-toed shoes, or if other people make their babysitters keep food logs while I merely leave a few bucks for pizza.

Fast-forward to my discovery of Taz's contraband, when it was more obvious than ever just how far I'd fallen short of Perfect Mommyhood. All my maternal failures were staring me in the face in the form of that little metal box filled with booze, condoms, and what-ever that green stuff was. I didn't know what I was going to do.

I decided to try my trusty source in all things, better than a priest, a shrink, a ghostbuster, or an encyclopedia, or any of the many parenting books I'd read over the years. My guru, my oracle, my goddess, my Google. Yes, I pray to the Temple of Google, for Google knows all.

I tried to sum up my problem in a sentence. Then I typed it into the search box on my computer: "I found contraband hidden in my child's room." Thank good-ness, 765,894 responses came back. I scrolled through the first few pages of hits until I found a Q&A from some family services agency. "I found a condom in my sixteen-year-old daughter's purse. What should I do?" wrote one mother. (Oh, if *only* Taz were sixteen . . .) The agency said it's probably a good thing that the girl is prepared for safe sex (here I perk up a bit) and warned the parent against assuming that the girl is already sexually active. Right, I said to myself, mustn't assume anything! Nevertheless, the website added, it's important for the parent to speak with the girl, warn against sexual activity at this age, and explain the risks and consequences. I have no problem saying what my rules are, and what the risks are. But where was the advice about how you deal with your kid's screaming and yelling over the fact that you went snooping in the first place?

I saw a way to send a question in, and so I clicked through and submitted my query. "Hi, I found liquor, condoms and an herb-like substance that I couldn't identify in a locked box in my thirteen-year-old's room, and he's going to be really angry that I was looking in his stuff. Do you have any advice?"

I clicked Send and then realized that I was a total moron. Not only would the vice squad be pounding on my door within minutes, not only had I jeopardized my family life and Taz's future, but I sounded like an idiot!

Then I formulated the answer to my own question in my head: "You don't have to justify anything! You are the mother! As long as your child is living under your roof, as long as he is a minor suspected of breaking the rules, you have the right to search, snoop, and confiscate!" The vice squad never came. Neither did advice from the website. It appeared I had sent my plea for help into a black hole.

I freaked out on my own for a few more days before

getting the courage up to tell Elon about what I'd found. He was, as usual when these parental crises occurred, sad and resigned. We are failures as parents, he sighed, doomed. And there's no point in doing anything. He thought it was pointless to take the stuff away, and said instead that we should just keep an eye on what's in the box. Who knows how that stuff got stashed in there, he added, or why, but maybe it'll still be there in a couple of months, untouched, and all this worry will be for nothing.

I decided to consult a friend who writes about parenting. Her kids are much younger than mine, but she reads a lot of books and talks to a lot of experts. And lo and behold, she had an idea that might work: Take the stuff away and leave a note in the lockbox expressing my concern.

It was a plan I could live with. Wimpy, yes, utterly cowardly. And yet at least I'd be doing something, rather than nothing. I confiscated the liquor and the herb, whatever it was. I left the condoms in there, with a note in the lockbox expressing my concern. "We need to talk!" I wrote in my loopiest schoolgirl script. "Love, Mom and Dad."

Before we knew it, the day arrived when Taz's plane was due home. I put all the worries about contraband out of my head, and told myself I'd deal with it at a later time. Right now, I was just going to concentrate on welcoming my son home from his once-in-a-lifetime trip Down Under.

I'm sort of embarrassed to admit that some of my

biggest fears for him going on that trip had to do with material possessions. I knew they could always be replaced, but among the many things that Taz had done to irk me during his thirteenth year was that he developed a tendency to lose things. He'd misplace his keys (like he did the day Sport put a bobby pin in the lock), lose the train pass he needed to get to school, and ask for help in finding his shoes. (They were always under the bed, of course, but he needed me to tell him that.) He missed deadlines at school, left his jacket at his friend's house, wasn't sure where his backpack was. If I gave him $10, it was gone in an hour, and he had nothing to show for it.

I knew several people who'd had their passports stolen on trips abroad, so I bought him one of those geeky document holders that you wear on a string around your neck, under your shirt, to keep the passport and his cash in, in the hopes that it would help insulate him from either his own carelessness or potential pickpockets.

I agonized about whether to send him with Australian currency, a debit card, traveler's checks, or a credit card, and finally decided that cash might be the easiest for him to keep track of and budget, even though it posed the risk that if he lost the money or were robbed, he'd be without a cent.

I gave him enough underwear and changes of socks so that he'd have clean clothes every day for half the trip. I hoped he'd figure out how to do his laundry at some point, but if he had to wear every item twice, I recognized that it wouldn't be the end of the world. I just hoped he didn't do like he did in Kansas, and spend days on end in the same pair of socks.

But truthfully, as I packed his bag—sending him off with a video camera, a digital camera, and an underwater camera for the Great Barrier Reef—I mentally kissed each item good-bye. I imagined he'd leave a trail of electronics at every hotel room between Canberra and Sydney. I tried to look at it philosophically, figuring that for a couple hundred bucks, they could all be replaced.

Besides, who knew if he'd even remember to charge them. Maybe he was going to end up standing in a eucalyptus forest, faced with a unique chance to take a photo of a koala bear, and find that the camera had run out of battery power. And, of course, since the voltage in Australia is different from here, I had to buy a converter in addition to an adapter.

But guess what? He came back with every single item he left home with. He got great video and great still photos of everything from kangaroos and crocodiles to Aboriginal street musicians and the Sydney Opera House. He even had underwater shots of the coral reefs. His passport was there, and he'd managed his money just fine, getting rid of all his Australian dollars before he returned and even coming home with $25 in U.S. cash. (In the interests of full disclosure, I should admit here that on a subsequent family trip, I was the one who lost the video camera, leaving it in a hotel room in Oregon, never to be found again. Obviously, I will never live this down with my children.)

But what was most remarkable to me about Taz's trip to Australia was that he came home with clean socks. It seems he'd done his laundry at some point and a few items were still unused. He didn't know how to do his laundry at home, but the fact that he could do it on another continent gave me hope for the future. I'd clearly underestimated the kid.

Then as we waited for his luggage, I heard an announcement over the loudspeaker in the terminal.

"Will the passenger who left a baseball cap on Flight Forty please return to the gate to get your hat?"

Yep, it was his. Five minutes on home soil and he was back to his old ways already.

We fetched the cap and then started asking him about his trip. He'd had a great time, of course, but he also seemed taller. And over the next few days, he seemed helpful around the house. He played nicely with his little brother. Some of the kids he'd been hanging out with before he left seemed to be gone from our lives.

Taz was still thirteen, but as he headed to the fourteenth birthday, just a few months away, he actually seemed slightly more mature.

And then a few days after he got home, I sensed him sort of staring at me with an amused smile. It was a strange expression and I didn't quite know what to make of it. Then I realized: He'd looked in the lockbox and found my "We need to talk" note, and he was waiting for me to say something.

I berated myself for my cowardice. I should have confronted him the moment he came home. Once again, I could only conclude that I was a Terrible Mother. But I just didn't have the guts to bring it all up out of the blue. I felt like Taz could read my mind, like he knew that I was thinking about this all the time, that every conversation we had about other things was actually false because there was a different conversation we were supposed to be having.

Finally, after what seemed like a long period of procrastination—although in reality it was only a day or two—the right moment presented itself. Sport was out of the room, but Elon and I were there.

"So I guess you know we found that stuff in your box," I said.

No reaction from him.

I proceeded with the Lecture that I'd been rehearsing in my mind, outlining the rules against drugs and alcohol, explaining the risks, and adding that if there was another incident like this, we'd all have to go to family counseling, with the money coming out of the fund for our next vacation. As for the condoms, I said I certainly hoped he wasn't going to need them until he was much older, but I had decided not to take them away because I wanted him to know that I considered safe sex important.

I looked at him, waiting for a response. I had expected

him to be furious, defensive, making a scene. But he was strangely quiet.

And what was that spreading over his face? A grin?

He was smiling! As if this whole thing was a joke!

"You think this is funny?" Elon asked angrily.

"I knew you'd go looking in there," Taz responded with a snicker. "So I left all that stuff for you to find."

"Oh come on," I said. "You don't think we're going to believe that!"

"No, really! I found that stuff in the park. I don't even know what it is. I just figured you'd find it and flip out while I was gone."

The grin on his face could only be described as shit-eating. But I wasn't laughing.

"You found a dozen wrapped condoms in the park? Right. You must think we're idiots!" I said.

"Oh, no, I found the bottles and the other stuff in the park. The condoms, they were giving those out at the gay pride parade. They were giving them to everybody, even little kids! I was walking down the street when the parade went by, so I collected a bunch of them. I'm going to dress up as Trojan Man for Halloween."

"Trojan Man?" I said. "You're kidding, right?"

"No, no, it's going to be really funny. Another kid I know is going to dress up as a birth control pill. Won't that be great? We'll go trick-or-treating together. It's going to be so funny!"

"OK, the Halloween costume is one thing, but the liquor . . ."

"I swear, I found it! The homeless people and the high school kids, they leave all kinds of crap in the park. I knew you'd go looking in my room, so I thought it would be funny if I put that stuff in there to freak you out."

He was laughing by then, high on his own demented cleverness. I looked at Elon. He was shaking his head and looking at the ceiling. He was not smiling.

Finally, he looked at our son. "You can't possibly expect us to think you're telling the truth," he said.

"Fine, don't believe it. But it's the truth." He looked at me blankly, the innocent look of a newborn who's just taken his first poop.

But I didn't know what to think, or say, or do. Of course it was absurd! Ridiculous! How could I believe this cockamamy bullshit!

On the other hand, the bit about the condoms at the gay pride parade and the plan to dress up as Trojan Man, well, it was so utterly juvenile that it actually seemed plausible.

Either way, though, whether it was true or false, Taz had outwitted me and I had no idea how to respond. Finally, I pointed out that none of the Perfect Mommies of our neighborhood were going to give candy to a hulking teenager covered in condoms; he'd be better off getting a chain saw and dressing up as a crazed murderer.

Just then, Sport called him from another room. He wanted Taz to come play Monopoly.

"I'm coming," Taz said, and off he went.

"So," said Elon, "how do you think our little talk went?"

"Um, good!" I said cheerfully. "We stated our values and we stated the rules. That's what we set out to do, and we accomplished our goals." I smiled sweetly and added: "And I think I gave him some really top-notch advice."

"About what?"

"About Halloween costumes."

# THE MYSTERIES OF GIRLS

Sometimes it seems like a cruel trick that I ended up with two sons, since I knew so little about the ways of boys when I became a mother. Not only did I spend my teenage years at an all-girl school, but I also grew up with a sister and no brothers. I practically didn't have a conversation with a boy my age until I went to college.

And yet somehow I am now a Lone Woman in a Land of Men, the only member of my household who won't walk around wearing nothing but underwear and who goes ballistic if the toilet seat is left up.

I am also the only one in my house who has no interest in watching, playing, or following sports in any way, shape, or form. And that's another one of those things from my childhood that has changed with the times—thank goodness. Like a lot of girls I knew growing up, I pretty much never caught or threw a ball, or watched an organized ball game, until my own kids started playing sports. I'm still mystified by the definition of a double play, and inevitably I am chatting with another mom or reading the paper when a Really Important Thing Happens in the game.

Which always leads Elon to come running over to loudly cross-examine me.

"Did you see what your son just did?" he'll demand after Sport—who is a very good athlete—has done something amazing. "Did you? You weren't paying attention, were you? Your son scored the winning goal"—or shot, or hit, or run, or pitch, or whatever they call it in whatever sport was being played—"and, as usual, you missed it."

I'm so pathetic, most of the time I can't even tell which team is winning, or whether our score is being tallied under "Home" or "Guest." I'll try to fake it, try to sound halfway intelligent and attentive by saying things at halftime or between innings like "So, how are we doing? Are we still—I mean, is the score, uh, still, you know, two to . . . uh, what is it now? I think I might have missed that last play when I had a sneezing fit. You know, I think I must be allergic to something out here in the field!"

Inevitably, my ploy only makes me sound more idiotic than ever. The score is never two to anything; it is always some improbable set of numbers that I couldn't begin to guess at, like fifteen to nothing, or tied six-six for the past forty-five minutes.

But it wasn't just sports where my knowledge of boys was deficient. So ignorant was I in the ways of boys that I naively thought, when Taz was little, that all gender differences were culturally imposed rather than inborn. I even got him a doll when he was about three, thinking, idealistically, that probably boys would love to play with dolls if only they had the chance. I showed him how to cuddle the dolly, hold it, rock it, and pretend to feed it.

"It's like your baby," I explained.

He immediately informed me that it wasn't a baby, it was a passenger on a train. He lined the dining-room chairs up and smashed the dolly down on a chair, then pretended to be the conductor, taking imaginary tickets and announcing imaginary stops.

Next, he went and got his little toy doctor kit and told me the dolly was sick. He proceeded to give it injections, take its temperature, wrap its leg up in a cloth bandage, and give it an operation. I'm fairly certain he was planning an amputation, but I managed to save the dolly before any limbs were severed.

All in all, he had a great time with that dolly, but he did things to it that I never would have dreamed of doing to a doll when I was little.

Despite this early and somewhat shocking introduction to the concept that Boys and Girls Really Are Different, gradually I came to love the Ways of Boys. And the more time I spent around Taz and his brother and their friends, the more I related to them, and the less I found myself able to relate to girls. Eventually, girls grew even more mysterious to me than boys had ever been.

For example, I loved the way boys carried out their friendships. There was no gossip, no meanness, no exclusionary behavior, no teasing or tattling. If they didn't like something, they'd just punch the other guy. And then, five minutes later, they'd be friends again. It was all so clear-cut.

In contrast, with girls, there was always a long, involved, complicated story involving alliances, nuances, guessing what the other one was thinking or saying behind your back, whispers, and tears.

I remember going on class trips with both my kids, and finding it so much easier to help corral the wild boys than to sort out all the emotional entanglements of girls. With boys, all you needed to do was yell at them to sit down and be quiet, stop throwing things, and quit poking the kid in the next seat.

But with girls, it seemed like one of them was always sitting alone in the corner of the bus crying, while a trio of her former best friends sat nearby giggling, giving her sidelong glances.

A few times, I was foolish enough to try to wade into this morass to make peace. "What's the matter?" I'd say, unleashing an unfathomable tale of double-crossing, sly insults, and betrayals. Eventually, I'd give up trying to make sense of it, and say something like "I don't understand. You girls were friends yesterday. Can't you just shake hands and be friends again? What's the big deal? Don't you see how silly this all is?"

It was quickly made clear to me that I was the one

being silly. No group of girls ever resolved their problems so straightforwardly, and somewhere in the back of my mind I began to remember my own complicated experiences with cliques and castes and judgments. I guess I'd tried to block it out after all these years, but, yes, somewhere at the edges of my memory, I do remember feeling weepy about being left out of this sleepover invitation or that round of phone calls about what to wear to school the next day.

Watching my boys and their buddies fall in and out of friendships with no hard feelings had allowed me to repress those painful memories of what being friends with other girls was really all about. It was totally different with male friendships, from what I observed. So what if they hadn't played with a certain kid in two years? If he was the only warm body around and they were short a man to get a game of street football going, hey, he was suddenly an old pal again, just like that.

A couple of mothers of girls I know also tell me that they all use instant messaging and MySpace pages to gossip about one another and say terrible, hurtful things. (And then there was the crazy case of the mother who pretended to be a kid, saying hurtful things to a teenage girl who eventually committed suicide.) Well, as far as I could tell, boys also insult each other online. But to them it's all a joke, or a competition even—an online version of the Dozens, the old insult-trading game that, in a more innocent era, began with "Your mother wears Army boots!"

There's even a website that automatically supplies "Yo mama" insults, or "snaps," as they call them. I've seen Taz and his friends sitting at computers, trading these downloaded lines at rapid-fire speed while laughing uproariously.

"Yo mama's so fat, she could sell shade! . . . Yo mama's so ugly, even a blind man wouldn't have sex with her! . . . Yo mama's so nasty, a skunk smelled her ass and passed out!"

OK, so they're not the most sophisticated jokes you've ever heard, but you can see how they might sound pretty funny if two thirteen-year-old boys were shooting them back and forth every thirty seconds.

In general, though, I do think mothers of boys have it easier than mothers of girls when it comes to making sense of friendships. And despite the phenomenon of sneakers that cost a hundred dollars and pants that show your boxers, I also think it's easier to be the mother of a boy when it comes to clothing.

I don't envy all the moms out there who have to police their daughters' necklines, bra straps, belly buttons, butt cracks, and skirt hem lengths. Things that my friends were embarrassed to be showing when they were thirteen, today most girls go out of their way to show.

"They want to look lascivious," one mother of a teenage girl said to me. Another merely said, "I feel sorry for the boys."

Arguing with girls over whether their clothing is too

suggestive makes my fights over Jordans look easy. But at least most schools have a dress code, so parents can always tell girls that what they're wearing is not going to pass muster at school. My son, on the other hand, will never be called to the principal's office because he spent too much money on his footwear.

While I am often shocked by the way thirteen-year-old girls dress, there have also been occasions when I have been moved to genuinely compliment a girl on what she's wearing. But my attempts to be nice never go over well. When a forty-something-year-old woman tells a thirteen-year-old girl, "Oh, I like your shoes!" or "Nice earrings!" she might as well be saying, "You are the most uncool person on earth. You look like you just walked out of a dressing room at Wal-Mart. You should strip on the spot, burn what you're wearing, and cover yourself with a sackcloth."

Of course, the girls that I've made the mistake of complimenting have all been too polite to run shrieking in the other direction. But even their subdued thank-yous were not enough to hide the looks of sheer horror on their faces. Clearly, there can be no greater insult to an adolescent female than to have a middle-aged woman like your style. I can only imagine how many perfectly fine pieces of jewelry, sweaters, jackets, and boots have been discarded by girls in Taz's circle, simply because I couldn't keep my mouth shut.

As divine punishment for my insensitivity toward the clothing codes of teenage girls, the good Lord sent me word of my very own thirtieth high school reunion. Immediately upon being told of the date of this momentous event, I started obsessing about what to wear. How could I prove that I was no longer as uncool as I once had been? And what about my gray hair? My wrinkles?

Well, after long deliberations (not to mention thoughts of changing my name and moving to Costa Rica), I finally decided on the perfect outfit. Then my friend Linda arrived from out of town to go to the party with me and announced right off the bat that my planned outfit—brown corduroy jeans that make me look really skinny and a really cute brown suede jacket—was totally wrong.

"Corduroy?" she said incredulously. "You're wearing corduroy pants in June with a brown suede jacket? You'll die of heatstroke."

Glumly, I realized she was right. It was one of those hot, sticky days with about 110 percent humidity. If I wore what I was planning to wear, I would be drenched in sweat and passing out before I even got to the party. Linda was unhappy with her own choice of shoes for the event, so we set out to go shopping, and I figured maybe I'd buy something else to wear.

We went to a few stores, and she bought better shoes. I bought a few things, too, but when I got home I realized that one of the tops I'd bought was too trendy, and I didn't want to look like I was trying to act too young, while the other one wasn't trendy enough, which was even worse.

Suddenly, it hit me that getting ready for my high school reunion was making me feel like I actually was in high school again. I suppressed the urge to scream, "Oh my God, I HATE myself!"

I tried to get a grip, went back to my closet, and somehow managed to find something suitable to wear. But it was plain and boring and not really all that stylish. Just like how I dressed when I was back in high school. At least my pants weren't too short (now that short pants are in).

Then I looked in the mirror and realized that the problem really wasn't with my clothes, it was with my hair. I'd dyed the gray out of it, but it was a frizzy mess, as it had always been. (And as we all know, sometimes when people say, "You haven't changed a bit," it's not a good thing.) But it was too late for a hair makeover; we had to be there in an hour.

The other problem was with my face. Since when did I have all those pouches and lines in my skin? Why had I thought it was a good idea to be suntanned when I was seventeen?

Then Linda slipped me the Magic Potion. No, it wasn't a drug or anything, it was wrinkle cream! Oil of Olay Total Effects.

"Wow, this really works," I said, a few minutes after applying it and convincing myself that I had fewer lines around my eyes than I had five minutes earlier. Problem was, I still had more lines around my eyes than I did when I graduated from high school.

We arrived to find several of our former classmates standing outside the appointed gathering place, smoking nervously. They were afraid to go inside, and so were we. Someone else from the class had promised Linda she was going to be early—the first one there! But, of course, when we finally got the nerve to walk in, she was nowhere to be seen.

Within a few minutes, however, more of our classmates had shown up, including another friend I'd stayed very close to over the years. She handed me a small bag when she saw me.

"It's a present," she whispered. "You'll love it."

Inside was another brand of wrinkle cream.

Hours later, after hugging everyone and talking so much that I literally lost my voice, when I looked around at my old acquaintances, I decided that most of us looked better than we had when we were teenagers— I suppose because most of us had found flattering hairstyles (except maybe for me) and could dress the way we wanted instead of how the crowd or our mothers dictated.

And truth be told, there were very few of these forty-something women who didn't still remind me of their young selves. The ones who were funny and clever still made me laugh; the ones who were serious and brilliant could still hold me in their thrall. I started thinking that maybe being a high school girl wasn't so bad after all— maybe we'd had a lot of fun amid all the social jostling and stress of the cliques.

It was only later that I realized almost none of the Cool Girls had attended the reunion. Does that mean reunions are basically for dorks? Well, if I was there, then maybe so . . .

I ended up corresponding with one of the Cool Girls by e-mail afterward. She confessed to me that being a Cool Girl in high school was very stressful in its own way, but she then pointed out that she actually hadn't been in the very Coolest Clique, she'd been in the Next-to-the-Coolest Clique.

All of which only made me realize that not only was I incapable of figuring out girls nowadays, but I couldn't even figure out the girls from my own generation. Girls, it seems, are just a mystery to me.

Which would explain why I was always puzzling over some behavior I'd observe among the girls in Taz's circle. I'd notice them doing something, but have no idea how to interpret it. It was like being a novice wildlife watcher and seeing some creature perform an apparently inexplicable act—like salmon trying to swim upstream, against the current—without having a clue as to why.

For example, the girls Taz knows have a habit of walking up to him and other boys to give them hugs. I don't think I will ever get used to seeing this, but it seems to happen every time I go to his school for a teacher conference or some other event. It's a wordless custom, from what I've observed, and there doesn't seem to be any other overt way in which they acknowledge knowing each other. No hi, no smile, no wave, no high-five—just the Hug.

Witnessing this interaction always makes me feel like I am a tourist in a country where I do not know the customs and cannot speak the language. Yes, I'm living in the Land of Thirteen-Year-Olds, and I sure wish I'd done more research before I ended up here.

And then there are the calls in the middle of the night. The phone rings a couple of times, just enough to wake you out of a sound sleep. But they hang up before you can actually pick up. These callers, Taz says, are always girls—usually girls at a slumber party daring each other to call boys.

I've thought about using the *69 callback feature to contact a few of their parents, but I don't want to be the grown-up version of a tattletale. So I decided that unless someone else's kid's behavior was causing chronic problems for me, I would let it go. It all seems to be an elaborate dance designed to attract attention from the opposite sex, but if you're really cool, you don't acknowledge that you've noticed anything.

Besides, for all the strutting I see on corners and subway platforms, for all the sexy screen names, profane MySpace messages, and flirtatious acts—like the wordless hugs and the calls in the middle of the night—it's not like anybody's wearing anybody else's ring, or going on a "date," or even making out in public places.

Clearly, these are mere preliminaries to more serious physical interactions and emotional entanglements, but as far as I can tell, for most thirteen-year-olds, it doesn't go much further than "grinding" parties, where they smash their (clothed) bodies against one another while loud pulsing music plays in the background. If a school-sponsored dance starts to go that way, the chaperones are instructed to physically break 'em up. The adults literally insert themselves in between the offending couples and warn them to find another way to enjoy the music. If a home party goes that way, you can only pray that the parent is on the premises and paying attention.

My personal parenting experience in this regard has been rather limited, due, I suspect, to an uncharacteristic discretion on my son's part. Like most wild creatures, the adolescents I see seem to do a good job of keeping their dating and mating habits secret. Or, as the ten-year-old younger brother of a couple of teenagers I know put it, "My brothers would never talk about girls at home!"

And in that respect, it may be the one way in which thirteen-year-olds do not act like eighteen-year-olds. Not yet, anyway.

Here's another sign that I've spent too much time with boys to understand girls. All over the country, thirteen-year-old girls are growing their hair long, in order to some day cut it off and mail it away to charity.

"Donate your ponytail!" the Locks of Love web-site cheerily urges on a page decorated with little red hearts. There are photos of bald kids juxtaposed with pictures of them wearing wigs, and photos of the donors, literally holding their chopped-off ponytails in their hands. Some girls grow their hair for years before making the cut.

Girls do this as a form of community service, the way other kids raise money for good causes or volunteer at a soup kitchen. But why does the very thought of it make me want to stick my finger down my throat and say, "Eeeewww!" Why does it seem so Karen Carpenter to me, so Joan of Arc?

I know, I know, these girls are doing such a good and kind thing, and giving of themselves in such a sweet, pure, and wholesome way. I would have thought that after all the years I've spent in the company of boys, with their burping contests, diarrhea jokes, whoopee cushions, and murderous video games, that I wouldn't be so creeped out by a disembodied chunk of hair.

But maybe I'm just so immersed in the culture of boys who want to be bad that I can no longer appreciate the innocence of girls who want to do good by literally giving away a piece of their physical selves. To me, Locks of Love can only fall into the category of "Mysteries of Girls," and I'd probably best leave it at that before my moral turpitude gets me in any more trouble than I'm already in.

Another big difference between the Ways of Boys and the Ways of Girls is how they do in school. When I was a kid, there was a lot of hand-wringing over gender differences in school, but the gender everyone was worried about was girls. Girls needed more encouragement in science and math! Girls needed to be club president, not club secretary! Girls needed to be playing on teams, not cheerleading!

But today the idea that girls need some extra advantage to succeed seems as old-fashioned as a manual typewriter. By almost every measure, girls today do better than boys—on standardized tests, in high school graduation rates, in acceptances to college. From early on, teachers say, girls work harder, and do better work.

Yes, I've seen the little girls reading Harry Potter books in kindergarten. I've observed them sitting nicely in their seats with their hands folded when the boys are running around the room like maniacs throwing spitballs. I can tell how much they love the many writing assignments in the early grades that now involve poems and journal entries. You see, I used to be one of those girls when I was little, reading big fat books with small print when I was seven, and writing tomes of prose by the time I was in fourth grade. And, yes, I did sit nicely while the boys ran around pitching paper clips up the substitute teacher's dress and stealing each other's hats. But somehow the boys never got in trouble for this.

And that, I think, is what has changed. The behavior and academic orientation of girls is now considered the model for normalcy. And when wild little boys don't conform, they are perceived as troublemakers and mediocre students. When I was little, the boys got away with murder. Now they get yelled at and have to sit down and be quiet and do their work.

A woman in my neighborhood named Louise Crawford writes a very funny column called "Smartmom" for the local weekly, *The Brooklyn Paper,* and one of my favorite columns she ever wrote was about the nightly battles she has had with her son since first grade over writing assignments.

Crawford recalled that he once refused to write about a memory in his writer's notebook.

"I don't have any memories," he said.

"Of course you have memories," she said.

"Not any that I want to write about for homework," he said.

I laughed out loud. That was my boys to a T! Once, when one of Sport's teachers told me at a parent-teacher conference that he needed to write more about his feelings, I actually argued with her about it.

"Why?" I said. "Why does he have to write about his feelings? The history of Western literature written by men has almost nothing to do with feelings. It's all plot, and violence! It's about war, and crimes, and action. It's not about feelings. Boys don't like to think about their feelings!"

At this moment, Elon was giving me the Evil Eye, which made me realize that I had just destroyed any potentially decent relationship we might ever want to have with this particular teacher. I quickly shut up, and pretty much never said another word to her about what I perceived as female standards for how a child might express himself on paper.

Sport always got low marks on his writing from her, but I would just tell him, "It doesn't matter. You write about whatever you want. Don't worry about whether other people like it. Dad and I will always love it."

The point is, though, that between the time I was a kid and the time my kids got to school, the education system had decided that it placed more value on behavior and achievements that came naturally to girls. I always wonder if part of why Taz never loved reading was because I kept forcing him to read all those insipid paperback series that they now foist upon elementary school students—pat little formulaic plots that ostensibly involved magic or mysteries.

By the time Sport was that age, though, I smartened up. When he resisted reading the formula fiction about whodunits and time machines, I bought him a series of biographies for children. He was just a nonfiction, nitty-gritty kind of a guy; he liked real stories about real people, so why not let him start early in a genre he could relate to. But it always cracked me up if someone asked him what he was reading, because he would inevitably say something like "I'm reading the biography of Albert Einstein," or "I've just completed the life story of Harry Houdini. Did you know he was a pilot as well as a magician?"

But that just shows that your first child is your guinea pig, and sometimes you can use your experience to do a better job with the next kid who comes along. I didn't know enough, when Taz was little, to tell him that if he didn't have any memories to write about for his journal entry assignments, he should just write about whatever the heck he wanted. And I didn't have the guts to say that if he couldn't get through another Junie B. Jones book, maybe he'd like a book about the Civil War better. I just assumed that the teachers were always right, and that school was not Taz's thing.

Little did I know that by the time he was thirteen, experts and researchers would be concluding that his entire generation of boys was doing badly in school, and they'd be trying to figure out why. Now, I'm no expert on education, but maybe, as a first simple step, we could just stop asking them to write about their feelings, and let them write, I don't know, an account of last night's Yankees–Red Sox game instead.

Sport once wrote a sixty-page account, in longhand, about waiting for the bus for an hour. It was so realistic, you really did feel like you were standing at that bus stop with him. And that wasn't necessarily a good thing. Inexplicably, the teacher told him he needed more detail in his work. Um, actually, I was thinking more plot might have helped. Is the content of what they're writing really so important that we have to micromanage it? Isn't it enough just to have them making grammatically correct sentences, practicing handwriting, perfecting their spelling, and creating a coherent narrative?

It's no surprise, given the gender differences in scholastic achievements, that some of New York City's best high schools are dominated by girls. One of these schools looks for kids with the highest reading scores on standardized tests. Girls do better than boys on those tests, so the school admits more girls than boys.

Another school has an excellent science program. Well, imagine my surprise when another mother informed me that on her tour of this school, she was astonished to see that most of the students in the labs were female. Why is this? she asked the school tour guide. "The boys don't want to work that hard," she was told. When I was in high school, schools were desperate to get girls interested in science.

I told a colleague at work I couldn't understand how it was that boys do so much worse in school than girls, and yet somehow boys end up running the world, anyway. Maybe that would make things easier for my son, but it didn't seem fair to the girls.

She assured me that change was afoot. "Boys may run the world right now, but when this generation of girls graduates from college, the boys better watch out, because the girls are going to take over."

I briefly considered grooming Taz to be a trophy husband for some powerful woman down the line. Maybe I should worry less about having him slog through Shakespeare and start getting him interested in pedicures?

Either way, despite my lack of insights into girls, I do feel that it's my duty as a mother to occasionally try to talk to my boys About Girls and Related Subjects, such as Sex. And yet you get to a point with these Important Talks where you don't know exactly what to say.

I mean, I've tried to be responsible over the years, but hey, once they know where babies come from, once they know what AIDS is, once they know what condoms are for, what's left? You told them, the school told them, ads on TV told them, and every other kid in the neighborhood told them. When you get down to the nitty-gritty, it's not all that complicated, and a parent can actually run out of talking points. My friend Vivian told me that the only questions her son Julian had left were either not about sex ("What is lactation?") or were not questions she was sure she knew the answer to ("How do gay people do it?").

Still, I figure when you have a teenager, it's irresponsible not to bring the subject up from time to time, even when you're pretty sure they already understand the basics.

"Taz, I need to have a little talk with you," I told him as he walked in the door on a Friday afternoon.

"Again? Didn't we just have one of these? Do we have to do it now? It might ruin my weekend," he said.

"Actually, I'm sort of hoping it will," I said.

"What do you mean?"

"Well, I just want to go over a few things about sex."

"Not again! I know everything I need to know."

"That's what I'm afraid of."

And therein lies the parent's dilemma. Do you really want to know the extent of your teenager's sexual knowledge? Not that they would tell you if you asked, but should you ask, and if you ask, what are you sup-posed to ask?

I took the coward's way out. I didn't ask. I just told.

"Taz, I hope you don't have sex until you're much older, and I hope when you do that it's with someone you love and not just because a bunch of people got drunk at a party or something."

I'd so far been avoiding eye contact, but there I paused for effect and tried to get my nerve up for the next pronouncement. I looked at him and he seemed completely unembarrassed by anything I'd said. I could have been telling him that he needed to work harder in geometry and he'd have had the same look on his face of utter nonchalance.

Finally, I took a deep breath and let out the next bit: "And I hope that you respect the girls you know and that if there's a girl who doesn't respect herself, that you don't take advantage of her."

Here he looked at me a bit quizzically. I could see that he wasn't 100 percent sure of what I was saying, but, frankly, I didn't have the guts to spell it out any more explicitly than that. But I had to try, and I had to do it in a most unfeminist way.

"You know, I am a girl," I said, not intending it to sound quite as dramatic as it did.

He shifted uncomfortably. "Yeah," he said.

"What I mean is, I was a girl. And I knew lots of girls. And sometimes girls can get boys into trouble. And then later they blame the boys. And since you are a boy, and I am your mother, I just want to make sure you don't do something stupid because of a girl."

Now he was knitting his eyebrows. "OK . . .," he said a bit tentatively.

Then he brightened, interpreting my pause as the end of our little chat. "Can I go now?"

I wasn't sure I'd made my point all that well. Maybe it was worth trying a different tack. "Um, just one more thing. I just want to remind you of the turkey story."

"What does that have to do with this? Besides, you don't have to remind me. I remember it."

"Too bad, I'm going to tell it again anyway."

Some families still use Bible stories to teach children right from wrong. But I like to use sensational tabloid headlines to hammer home my do-right lessons, and the turkey story is my all-time favorite. When the incident happened, I read the account from the paper out loud as we gathered around the dinner table, and I have brought it up at least once every few months in the three years since.

The turkey story is basically this: A group of teenagers used a stolen credit card to go on a shopping spree. Their purchases included a frozen turkey from a supermarket. They all got in a car, and one of them decided to pitch the turkey at another car. It smashed the windshield, injured the driver, and all of the kids were arrested.

Even though this is not directly related to sex, to me it seems to capture perfectly the idiotic behavior that groups of teenagers frequently engage in, and how, like sheep, they will follow one another, giggling and failing to use a shred of common sense, in doing the most inane and dangerous things. They can hurt themselves, they can hurt others, and the actions of one of them can get all of them arrested. It reminds me of every story I've ever heard of frat parties gone bad and teams getting in trouble, stories which not infrequently involve sexual misdeeds of various sorts.

So I retold the story and added, "The point is, you have to think for yourself. Just because a bunch of people are doing something stupid doesn't mean you have to go along with it. If one of those people gets in trouble, you will, too. Like at the prom, remember?"

"OK," he said, impressing me with how pleasant and sincere he sounded. "Can I go now?"

But the turkey story had emboldened me; now I had my second wind and suddenly felt like I could say what was really on my mind.

"Just one more thing; I promise this is the last thing I wanted to say. I just wanted to remind you about condoms . . ."

He interrupted me. "Oh, don't worry about that," he said. "Come in my room for a second."

What? "Come in my room for a second" is not the right response when your mother says she wants to talk to you about condoms. Now I was freaking out. Exactly what was it he was planning to show me? We walked down the hall together and into his room. He reached into a little wooden box on top of a shelf covered with a jumble of CDs, DVDs, deodorant, acne medicine, keys, candy, and empty water bottles.

"See?" he said. He pulled out a couple of NYC Condoms, the brand the city of New York created as a freebie to promote safe sex. The sleek black wrapper is designed to resemble the logo for subway lines, with each letter in NYC CONDOM pictured in a colorful little circle, the way the F train's *F* appears in an orange balloon on the front of the train and the A train's *A* is set in a circle of navy blue.

He smiled and looked at me expectantly, the way our dog, Buddy, looks when she sits on command or puts her paw up to shake. She knows she did a good job, she's proud of herself, and now she wants a treat.

I reminded myself that I brought up the subject of condoms, and here he was showing me, like the good boy he thought I wanted him to be, that he had some.

I suppose this shouldn't have shocked me. After all, we'd already been through the incident with the Halloween condoms, which did, in fact, disappear after October 31 that year—whether in service of a costume or an orgy I guess I'll never know for sure. But I hadn't realized that the supply had been replenished. I was about to stutter, "Where did you get them?" but then I remembered that when these NYC Condoms had been introduced a few weeks earlier, the condoms were handed out in subway stations and on street corners.

People even brought them in to show around the office that day. After that, you could pick them up in bars and many other places around the city, even coffee shops and hair salons. So I knew they were easy to find even in our neighborhood, but I was still a little taken aback.

Before I had a chance to say anything, though, he offered an explanation, saying that when the city started handing them out, his friend Chris picked up a whole bunch and gave him a couple.

"Now can I go?" he said.

"Uh, sure," I said. "I guess I've said everything I wanted to say."

"Great," he said. "Bye, Mom, see you later."

The apartment door slammed behind him and I resisted the urge to walk over to the window and watch him go—or even follow him—down the block to hang out who knows where, with who knows who, doing who knows what.

A few days after Taz and I had our little chat, Elon came storming into the kitchen where I was making one of those special dinners I get all proud of, and then want to kill myself because no one will eat it. This one was a lovely stir-fry of chicken and asparagus, but as I peeled the ginger, I could already imagine Taz conspiring with Sport to microwave some Bagel Bites when I wasn't looking.

"Do you know what your son has in his room?" Elon said.

"Let me guess. Ten pounds of dirty laundry from the last twenty-four hours? A history paper with a big C written on it in red ink?"

"Condoms! And they're not the ones we found last summer that he said were for the Halloween costume."

"No, these are the NYC Condoms that have those subway train designs on them, right?"

Elon looked horrified. "You know about this?"

"Well, yeah. I was giving him a little sex ed lecture the other night because, well, I don't know, somehow it seemed like the right time, and he showed them to me. He says he got them the day they were giving them out all over the city. There are two in there, right? Why don't you check again in a couple weeks or whatever and see if they're still there?"

Elon sighed. "OK."

It was so easy to pretend to be calm about this and talk the talk, like the reasonable parents we were trying to be. But inside, both of us were wishing that we didn't have to be thinking about these things with regard to a thirteen-year-old.

It's like they said on *South Park:* "There's a time and a place for everything. It's called college."

But, in reality, it starts long before then.

# 9

## EPIPHANIES

It was a big relief to leave the mess that was eighth grade behind us, and start fresh with ninth, in a place where none of the teachers knew anything about Taz. Or about the famous soda can incident. Or about the prom.

I tried to be optimistic that everything would work out OK in his new school. I told myself he would learn a lot, and hopefully be happy, and hopefully make friends with kids who would be a good influence on him.

But I was well aware that he had a few months to go before he stopped being thirteen. And, inside, I worried that the final stretch of this unlucky number might be just as bumpy as what we'd already been through.

As I explained before, where we live, there are no neighborhood high schools. Even ordinary public school students like Taz have to apply to high schools—just like college—and hope they are accepted at the school of their choice. It's a complicated system, with dozens of schools to choose from, in which the best schools look at your grades, your standardized test scores, and your attendance.

In addition to all of that, at Taz's first choice of a school, they also looked at teacher recommendations and a portfolio of work, and you had to come in for an interview and write an essay on a surprise topic. Elon and I were certain that Taz would never be accepted at this school. It was just too popular, and he was competing against kids with résumés that could get them into Harvard at the age of thirteen, forget high school. When we went for a tour, there was a line down the block, and by the time we got to the door, the person who greeted us apologized because she'd run out of maps. "We only printed a thousand," she said.

As charming as Taz could be (when he wanted to, that is, and only with people who weren't his parents), we knew he wasn't going to go in there for the interview and discuss poetry or physics. He plays no instrument, has no hobbies, and hasn't been on a team since he was a nine-year-old Little Leaguer who ducked every time the ball came within ten feet. If you ask him, "Who do you admire?" he'll say the guys in *Wedding Crashers*.

And yet he has a certain charm. He is cool and confident. He has a lot of friends. He is suave, like James Bond without the spying. I can't take credit for any of this; he's been that way since he was a little kid. In fact, it's one of the humbling—dare I say nerve-racking—aspects of being a mother that your kid's personality is a function of nature, not nurture. I read somewhere once that as long as you feed them and don't lock them in a closet, most of them will turn out fine, and we're just deluding ourselves to think that all the fine-tuning and obsessing we do makes any difference. Maybe Taz's inborn charm would allow him to jump through the hoops; certainly, if he aced the interview, it would have nothing to do with me.

Interview day arrived. Elon and I wished him luck and watched him walk in. He seemed totally nonchalant about the whole thing, but we were ready to throw up.

A half hour later, he emerged from the school, beaming.

"I'm in!" he announced in the cocky tone that can only be voiced by an adolescent who hasn't lived long enough to be disappointed by life's randomness.

Elon rolled his eyes. "Right," he said.

"You're in?" I said. "How could you possibly know that? It'll be months before they tell us if you've been accepted."

"I just know," he said. He folded himself into the car, bouncing his knee, a grin on his face, stuck his iPod buds in his ears, and shut his eyes. If Elon and I were a TV station, Taz had just changed the channel.

But I had to smile at his sheer hubris. God, it's great to have no self-doubt! I wish I could be that way sometimes. Then I reminded myself that it's attitudes like that that lead adolescents to indulge in Dangerous Risk-Taking Behavior! Like Failing to Put on Seat Belts! Riding Motorcycles Too Fast! Taking Ecstasy, Even! Not that

Taz had done those things, mind you, but they are all among the ten thousand things I make lists of when I can't sleep.

Later, a girl we know who attends the school Taz was applying to asked Taz what the surprise essay topic had been.

"You were supposed to write about a memory," he said.

Uh-oh, I thought, not the "write about a memory" assignment again! I hoped he hadn't frozen up, like the kid in the newspaper column who told his mom he didn't have any memories.

"So what did you write about?" the girl asked.

"I wrote about the time my uncle took me to a Mets game," Taz said.

"That was a mistake," she said. "You should have written about someone who died!"

"My uncle *did* die!" Taz said.

I marveled how the both of them had intuitively understood that the assignment wasn't *really* about a memory. It was really about whether you have Soul. Pity the kid who's had nothing but happiness in life and has no dead relatives to write about. A kid like that, writing about his first pony ride or some other wonderful moment from childhood, doesn't stand a chance in an essay exam these days.

Still, even though Taz appeared to have understood what was being sought in an essay topic, and thought he did well in the interview, the school seemed like a reach.

For a second choice, I insisted that he put a school I was certain he'd be accepted to—one that I liked, but he didn't. (Yes, my thirteen-year-old needed a safety school. Back in my day, you didn't need a safety school until you were applying for college.)

At one minute after three o'clock on notification day, my office phone rang.

"Mom?" he said, his voice small and sad. "I got into number two. The one you wanted."

I hated myself. I suddenly realized what a stupid thing I had done. "I'm so sorry," I said.

"Just kidding!" he shouted boisterously. "I got into you-know-where!"

"WHAT? No way! Are you sure? Read me the letter! I don't believe it!"

He read the letter aloud, and it seemed indisputable that indeed he had been accepted to his first choice. He had been right that day after the interview when he told us he was in. He had been right not to doubt himself. And to tell the truth, I felt bad that the doubts had come from us.

Maybe, I thought, just maybe, things would work out for Taz after all.

In the months that followed, the summer of Taz's thirteenth year came and went, and with it, the trip to Australia and the discovery of contraband in Taz's room, along with the usual "I Am a Terrible Mother" self-pronouncements. Then, finally, after Labor Day, high school began. Thank GOD! He would be someone else's worry, at least for a few hours each day.

I offered to accompany him to the building the first day, but he had no interest in being delivered to high school by his mother. He said he'd have no trouble figuring it out on his own. The first day was only a half day and he promised to call me when it was over.

When he reached me, he sounded positively jubilant. Our conversation went something like this.

TAZ: Mom?

ME: Hi, Taz, how was the first day?

TAZ: Awesome! I signed up for tennis, bowling, Frisbee, skiing, and the trip to France.

ME: What? Did you actually make it to school today, or did you get lost on the train and end up at a country club?

TAZ: No, see, these are all afterschool activities.

ME: A trip to France is an afterschool activity?

TAZ: Well—

ME: And by the way, I thought you were taking Spanish! How come you're signed up for the trip to France?

TAZ: Oh, don't worry, I signed up for the trip to Cuba, too.

ME: Cuba? It's not even legal to go to Cuba!

TAZ: It would be for educational purposes, or something like that.

ME: Right, speaking of educational purposes, were there any educational purposes related to your trip to school today? Things like, oh, I don't know, math? English? Social studies? Science? You know, the *in*school activities. As opposed to the *after*school activities?

TAZ: Oh, math and all that? We didn't get to that today. That stuff is happening tomorrow. But I'm just so happy! This is such a mad fun school!

Yes, it definitely sounded like a mad fun school. But does trigonometry happen at mad fun schools? Does World War I get studied? Or would that be too boring for a mad fun school? I was beginning to worry.

The next day, Taz came home and said that his English teacher was starting them on SAT words. Every kid had to bring in a word that might appear on the SATs, and teach it to the class. And you'd get brownie points if you could use the SAT word in a sentence, or if other people did, during class discussions.

Taz asked if I knew any good SAT words. I was pretty sure I hadn't started studying for the SATs when I was in ninth grade; in fact, I'm not even sure that I knew what the SATs were when I was in ninth grade. But I recognized that the teacher was doing the right thing in building their vocabulary well in advance of the exam, and I thought hard for a minute about a good word for Taz to share with the class.

Suddenly, one popped into my head, along with an image of my old English teacher, Mrs. Laster, and some vague recollection of her using this word to make a point about a James Joyce story.

"Epiphany," I said triumphantly. "That's a great word. Your teacher will love it."

"Epiphany? What's that?"

"It's when you're trying to understand something, and then, all of a sudden, you get it, and you're so excited, it's like you had a vision. It's when you realize something, but not gradually. You figure it out all at once, so it's almost like it was revealed to you. You understand?"

He nodded. He seemed kind of into it. "Epiphany," he repeated. "I think I get it. It's cool." He grinned.

Over the next few days, Taz had more epiphanies than Sir Isaac Newton. There were epiphanies about cheats in Halo, epiphanies about the dog, epiphanies about pizza. And Taz said that when it was his turn to teach his SAT word, the entire class had an epiphany about the word *epiphany*. It was a word that described an experience they'd all had, and it was especially useful in English class. The teacher would ask a question about why Holden Caulfield said or did a certain thing, and some kid would inevitably raise his hand to answer, calling out, "I just had an epiphany about that!"

I guess when you are thirteen, epiphanies just pop up in your brain all the time, like dandelions on a lawn. By the time you are forty, though, your reflexes are sufficiently slowed, and your knowledge of the world sufficiently broad, that an epiphany is about as rare as drinking whole milk.

But, eventually, I did have an epiphany. It was about Taz's relationship to his mad fun school. He was going every morning, and coming home every afternoon, but there didn't appear to be any epiphanies related to homework. "Don't worry about it," he'd say, night after night, when I asked about homework, after observing that none was getting done. "It's under control."

Even the activities he'd signed up for that first day had mysteriously evaporated. Bowling, he claimed, turned out to be stupid. Tennis was for people who were practically tennis pros. There was hardly any snow that winter, so the ski trip didn't happen, and the Frisbee team practiced at dawn, which is Taz's least favorite time of day. As for the trips, well, I couldn't afford to send him to France or Cuba—or North Korea, for that matter—so soon after Australia.

About a week before his fourteenth birthday, we got the first report card. The epiphanies flowed fast and furious as I surveyed all those Cs and Ds. Oh, I almost forgot—there was one B. For drama! Wait, let me share with you the epiphany I had about the B he got in drama: Taz is Good at Acting. As in Acting Like an Idiot!

What he did not appear to be good at was a much longer list, a list that included English, history, math, science, and Spanish. Also known as Every Single Subject That Matters.

The day after the report card came home was my flashback nightmare to the old Worst Night of the Year scenario, also known as parent-teacher night. Reluctantly, I dragged myself up to Taz's mad fun school for a meeting that I knew would be anything but mad fun.

There was only one good thing about parent-teacher night at Taz's new school. Instead of having you go from teacher to teacher, to hear six different people tell you how awful your child is, you only meet with one person, the child's adviser, who has collected reports from the other six about how awful your child is.

What's good about this is, it takes a lot less time than the other way, when you have to go from room to room hearing the same horrible stories over and over again. And also, this way, you only have to be polite to one person who thinks you are a Terrible Mother, instead of to a half dozen.

But what was good about the old system, where you did see all these different teachers, was that in each case you could act totally surprised by the news that your child is a screwup. You could sort of hint, or imply, that your child wasn't doing nearly as badly in the other classes. You could even say sly things that suggested, without really saying so, that maybe it's the teacher's fault that your child is doing badly in this particular class, because, well, it goes without saying that he might be doing OK in the other classes.

Of course, it goes without saying because you can't bring yourself to say it, because it would be a Total Lie.

So, instead, you resort to saying things that are slightly misleading, yet face-saving, without being Utter Crap. Things like "Well, you know, I think his major interests probably lie elsewhere—history's not really his thing," and "Huh, I guess he just doesn't have an ear for foreign languages—some people don't, you know," or "It's funny, I was never very good at math either, and when he asks me for help, I'm just *clueless*."

What's bad about the system where you only see one person is that you really can't get away with all this equivocation. You walk into that room, the adviser has evidence from six teachers to make her case about your child. You can't pretend there are no patterns. There's no place to hide.

And in Taz's case, the pattern was clear. He wasn't doing his homework. He wasn't studying for tests. He wasn't learning the material. About the only thing he was doing right was that he was showing up for class. Thank goodness for small miracles—at least he wasn't a truant! Although apparently when he got there, he forgot to turn his brain on. At least there were no complaints about the type of disrespectful behavior that got him in so much trouble in eighth grade. No soda cans, no confrontations, no calling teachers a "retard."

There was one nervy attempt to backpedal, however. After the adviser went over the reports from pretty much every teacher about how Taz hadn't turned any homework in, he began to insist that he had actually done all the homework, but he'd left it on the floor of his room.

For all the assignments.

In all his classes.

The adviser just stared at him for a moment. "I guess the floor of your room is a pretty messy place, huh?"

. Taz nodded and smiled idiotically, and the meeting went even further downhill from there.

The grades were so bad, and the conference was so depressing, that Elon was pretty much stunned into silence. You have to understand something about Elon. He is the smartest person I have ever met, but unlike some people who are really smart, he doesn't think everyone around him is stupid. In fact, he thinks the opposite. He starts out assuming that everyone else is smart, too, so it's always a terrible disappointment for him to find out that the rest of us can't multiply four-digit numbers in our head. We don't all know the population of every country in the world. We can't all convert kilometers to miles, Fahrenheit to Celsius, and euros to dollars. If he were a dog, he would win the Stupid Pet Trick contest every time, but the problem is, he wants the rest of us to win the contest with him, and we just can't.

Plus, he went to Yale. He was number two in his law school class. His brain is so big that we have entire teams of people playing Boggle against him, but even when two grown-ups and four kids add up all their scores, we still can't beat him. We're all making lists of words from the board like *hat* and *pen*, and he's offering up words like *conundrum*. We had to give up playing Scrabble because if you came up with a crappy word, he'd want to look at your letters and help you find a better one. Even when the only letters available were Q and Z, he could think of words *(quiz)*. Eventually, we realized he had memorized a Scrabble dictionary when he was eight.

So to have a son getting Cs and Ds—this was a terrible letdown. He was quiet and sad, shaking his head and sighing. I could see the question going through his head over and over again: "What are we going to do with this kid?" I had the same question, and no answer, so I couldn't think of anything to say to make him feel better.

But in addition to dealing with Elon's reaction, I had to deal with the adviser's reaction, which was, quite simply, to tell me that it was my responsibility to make sure Taz did his homework.

How was I to do this? Well, the school had a website, and most of the teachers put their assignments on it, so you could never say you lost the assignment or you were out sick as an excuse for not doing your work. The adviser told me that when a kid wasn't doing well, it was the parent's job to log on to the website every night and download the child's homework, then check each subject individually to make sure he had completed it.

I found this advice somewhat shocking. I had been under the impression that the trend now among educators is that they want parents to back off. I had read in *The Wall Street Journal* about how some students, when they get a bad grade, hand their cell phones to professors and ask them to explain it to their parents, and how college grads now bring their parents along to job interviews.

I just couldn't imagine myself fetching Taz's assignments each night, and I had incorrectly assumed that high school teachers wouldn't want me to. I had thought that they do not like so-called helicopter mommies, who hover over their darling's every misstep and try to fix it. I had naively been led to believe that it was better, at this age, to let your kid figure out how to solve his own problems, or allow him to suffer the consequences, rather than intervene and solve his problems for him.

OK, I did make a fuss when the middle school said Taz couldn't come in to pick up his report card. But hey, when he dropped his cell phone in the toilet, no way did I run out to buy him a new one. (Instead, I went out and celebrated with Elon, because we realized we were going to save so much money now that Taz wasn't racking up cell phone charges, we could now afford to go out to dinner!)

When confronted with the bad grades, it seemed to me that this, too, was Taz's problem to solve. I could, in fact, do as the adviser recommended, and check the high school website every night for his assignments, then demand to see them in order to confirm that they were done.

But really, I just didn't want to go there, and I didn't want to go there for all kinds of reasons, the most important of which is that I already went to ninth grade. And when I was in ninth grade, I did all my homework. And my mother didn't even have to check it for me. I really just don't feel like it's fair to make anyone on this earth responsible for ninth grade more than once in a lifetime.

Besides, once you check for the homework, and demand to see that it's done, you are bound to follow through by screaming and yelling or devising some type of punishment if it's not done. And the problem with Taz and punishment is that it never works. He's like Steve McQueen in *The Great Escape*. You can take everything away from him, and throw him in a dark cell over and over, and it just doesn't matter. If he wants to break rules and get out from under your thumb, he'll find a way to do it.

There have been times in the past where it seemed like Taz really had nothing left to lose—I'd taken away his money, TV, movies, video games, computer games, and time with friends—and he still refused to reform. About the only thing I didn't do was throw the switch on the fuse box and leave him sitting in the dark. (I actually considered that, but the refrigerator is on the same circuit and I didn't want to deal with the spoiled food.)

So it seemed to me that not only was I not personally motivated to monitor this homework business intensely, but I also wasn't sure how to discipline him if he failed to do as I asked. Smacking him was definitely out, by the way—he was way too big by then, and I didn't want to hurt my hand.

But there was another reason, too, beyond my lack of interest in reliving ninth grade and my inability to dole out effective punishments. I didn't want Taz doing the homework solely to avoid getting hassled by me. I wanted Taz to want to do well in school for reasons that had nothing to do with parental approval. I realized that was pie in the sky to some extent, but he had been a good student for most of middle school, at least until the dreaded thirteenth birthday. He knew how good it felt to get an A. I wanted him to want that feeling for himself again. I didn't want him to only get the A (though I would gladly settle for Bs) for me.

The thing is, I have lived long enough on this earth to know that when you do a good job, most of the time, no one is going to notice. No one is going to pat you on the back, or buy you a drink, or give you a raise, or arrange a parade. But if you did the best you could do, and if you are pleased with the result, that is something in and of itself that can give you a certain peace and satisfaction and happiness. It sounds trite to say, but a job well done is its own reward. And that's what I wanted Taz to feel. "Big Mother Is Watching You" did not hold much appeal to me as a slogan for child rearing.

Now, I didn't have the nerve to tell the adviser that I was not actually planning on getting all that involved in the homework checking, nor was I planning to devise some type of torture to compel Taz to do better in school. So I just nodded politely and promised to talk with Taz some more when we got home.

And talk I did. I basically told him there was no Plan B. I knew he loved this school, but I told him that I didn't think I could leave him there if he couldn't get better grades, because he'd never get into college.

But if he wasn't going to stay at his mad fun school, I wasn't sure where he was going to go. There is a high school near our home, but it is a rather scary place, with a high dropout rate. Once, when Taz was little, still in a stroller, we were walking up the block past that school, and a chair came flying out the third-story window, glass breaking and everything. Luckily, no one was injured on the street, but it was a terrifying moment. I reminded Taz that he didn't want to end up at a place like that.

Nor, I casually mentioned, did he want to end up in military school. Taz didn't know what military school was, so I explained it. It was a concept that had been prominently featured in one of *The Sopranos* episodes that Elon and I greatly enjoyed watching together, the one where A.J. got expelled from school, and Tony said to Carmela: "No more fucking schools that coddle him."

When they went to tour a military school, Carmela told a school official: "I do not agree with this hard-nosed discipline."

"Mothers seldom do," the official said.

At this point in our viewing of the episode, Elon turned to me and said, "See?"

"See what?" I said in an indignant tone of voice.

"Well, you're always making excuses for him!"

"OK," I admitted, "I'm a wimp when it comes to

punishment. But I don't see you coming up with a magic solution!"

If you are married and have children, I'm sure I don't have to continue this conversation for you, because you've probably had one just like it at some point in your family life. Or maybe, as with us, every day is *Groundhog Day* and like in the movie, you keep having the conversation over and over again but never manage to solve the problem of how to discipline your children.

Meanwhile, back in *The Sopranos* episode, Carmela was questioning the official about the school's approach. "What about creativity? Independent thought?" she said.

"We've created too many options for our kids," the official responded.

But options in my world were in short supply as I contemplated what to do with Taz if he couldn't hack it at this high school. One idea I mentioned to Taz was the possibility of going to live with his grandma, who has a perfectly nice high school in her town that anyone can go to as long as they live there.

Taz loves his grandma; they have a special bond. But leaving our neighborhood to live with her was not all that appealing as a solution to the high school crisis. I mean, maybe Taz wouldn't have minded leaving his parents and his brother, but there is no way he was leaving the dog. And his grandma definitely had no interest in adopting Buddy.

Although I had pretty much made up my mind that I couldn't get as involved in the homework as the adviser had suggested, I still worried whether I had made the right decision. I talked to a lot of other mothers, but they were not always comforting. Some were far less involved than I was, and the results were scary—kids flunking classes, going to summer school, sometimes being sent away to alternative schools.

On the other side of the coin, some parents were way more involved than I was, keeping track of assignments the way Taz's adviser had suggested, and guiding their kids to activities in order to "build résumés" in anticipation of college applications that were still more than three years away.

When I talked to parents of younger kids, they nodded sympathetically, but I could tell they thought I was one of those Degenerate Moms with Matching Kid. They simply could not imagine their own darling nine-year-olds, whose homework assignments came home covered in smiley-face stickers from the third-grade teacher every day, getting a D in school.

But when I talked to parents of older teenagers, they practically laughed in my face, saying things like "Ha! Wait until he takes the car without your permission and you have no idea where he is!" or "You think it's bad now, in a few years you'll be up at three a.m. every night, just like you were when they were babies, only this time you'll be waiting up for him, thinking he's been murdered outside a dance club."

The parents whose kids were in their early twenties also told scary stories. High school was ancient history to them; they were more interested in college night-mares and postcollege horror stories.

There were the Kids Who Refused to Graduate, who just kept enrolling semester after semester at colleges around the country, generating tuition bills from New Hampshire to New Mexico.

And there were also the Kids Who Came Home After College, who couldn't—or wouldn't—get jobs to match their degree in obscure things like ceramic arts.

Even some of the success stories were hard to bear, like the twenty-three-year-olds who were already earning twice what I earn or more. Inevitably, they worked at Wall Street firms, in jobs with titles like "trader" and "consultant." What exactly they did every day when they got to their offices, I had no idea.

There was one story of an older kid, though, that did make me feel better—enormously better—and I held his mother's words in my mind for months after Taz got the Bad Report Card. This mother's son was in many ways far more difficult than mine. He was a brilliant boy, but he couldn't cope with school. He eventually dropped out and got his GED. I had long admired the fact that rather than excoriating the kid, his parents had recognized how unique his situation was, supported his decisions, and never wavered in their love for him.

Both parents have advanced degrees from presti-gious universities, so I could only imagine how hard it was for them to explain to friends and relatives that their son was not going to college. Their faith in their child was eventually rewarded, however. He was a computer whiz, and at an age when most kids are still working on getting a degree, he got a job at a high-tech firm where what you know is far more important than how you did in school. In short order, he was earning a good salary, had a nice lifestyle, and loved his job. His parents were bursting with pride, and rightfully so.

I wondered if I'd have the mettle to stick up for Taz, the way they did with their son, if he didn't end up taking the conventional path through school.

But something the computer whiz's mother said stuck with me. She and her husband had sought help from a therapist in dealing with their unusual son, and she told me that the therapist had convinced her that it was not the parents' job to serve as rules enforcer for the school.

Yes, you can help with homework if your son asks, and you can create a schedule that sets aside a reasonable amount of time each day to do homework, but you are not the homework policeman, this mother explained. Your job is not to check each night to see that it is done. If they don't do their schoolwork, they have to deal with the consequences, even if the consequences mean failure.

What *is* the parents' job, she said, is to make sure that kids grow up to be decent, independent, fully functioning human beings.

So simple, and yet so overwhelming. It's actually easier to be the homework policeman than to play Pygmalion and shape a soulless lump of clay into a good person. How had I done so far? I asked myself. Well, Taz was definitely independent—I had succeeded a little too well in that department—but was he a decent human being?

I thought so. I hoped so. I know that he gives his seat up on the subway to old people and little children. I know that he is kind to animals. I know that he would give his last dollar to a homeless person, but is that good or naive? He was sometimes mean to his brother, but on the other hand, if Sport was having a problem with a kid on the playground, I could always dispatch Taz to go down there and straighten out whatever it was. He did call that teacher in middle school a retard, and that wasn't very nice. But maybe that was an isolated incident? Maybe he'd matured a little since then?

Either way, I thought about that mother's advice for months after the Bad Report Card. I wasn't the Homework Policeman, I reminded myself. I was merely in charge of raising a good person. You could say it was an epiphany.

I could only hope Taz would have his own epiphany about his mad fun school. He might be a decent human being, and maybe I Am a Terrible Mother, but if he was going to stay at this school, he was going to have to start checking the homework assignments on his own.

One night, there was a meeting at his school about how parents could help new students adjust. I told him, quite innocently, that I was planning to go to it, only to see a look of utter panic on his face.

"OH MY GOD, Mom, PLEASE, please, promise me you won't go," he responded. "That would be SO embarrassing!"

"How would that be embarrassing? I already went to your school one time to talk to your adviser about your grades, remember? Think about how embarrassing that was for me—my son, the kid with all the Cs and Ds! So why would it be embarrassing for you if I went to one of these meetings where nobody's even going to know I'm there?"

"Well, you know, because you're my MOTHER! Don't you get it?"

No, I didn't get it. He also didn't want me to go to the school auction, or the school play, or the school "get to know the principal" breakfast. Apparently, merely having to acknowledge in a public place that I exist, that he is not an orphan living in a cardboard box under the West Side Highway, but that he in fact has a mother who cares deeply about his future, would be enough to cause him complete and total humiliation.

Then I remembered that after Taz was born, Elon called his own mother up and apologized for refusing to walk next to her when he was an obnoxious teenager who didn't want anyone to know that he had a mother. Holding his newborn son made him realize how hurtful it must have been to be rejected by the child you devoted yourself to all those years. Maybe, if I am very lucky, some day Taz will have that same epiphany when he is a father—many, *many* years from now.

In the meantime, I was going to go to that meeting whether he wanted me to or not. I wimped out on telling him about it, though; I pulled a Jackie O, wore big sunglasses and a scarf around my head, and slunk into the cafeteria without signing the parent attendance sheet. As I arrived, a mother was relating to the dean a story that sounded like it could have come from the Annals of Raising Taz.

"My son seems like a fairly smart boy, and so do most of his friends," she said. "But they keep getting Cs on everything. They just don't want to seem to work hard enough to do well. What should I do?"

The dean said this was a phenomenon that he'd often seen, especially among male freshmen. He counseled that the first year of high school was a difficult transition for many kids from middle school, and that even most of the underachieving boys did much better as time went on.

Well, at least I wasn't the only one with this problem, and maybe, if the dean was right, I had reason to be hopeful that things would improve.

# THE SECRET LIVES
# OF TEENAGERS

**O**ne of my favorite conversations to have with other parents is about how they did all sorts of bad things when they were teenagers, and their parents never knew.

But now that they are parents, they are certain that their own teenagers never do anything wrong.

This makes getting real advice about how to deal with a teenager who is doing something wrong next to impossible, because nobody will admit to having that sort of teenager—unless, of course, they get a call from school or the cops. At which point it's too late to get advice from other parents because the way forward will pretty much be mandated by a judge or a principal.

Are teenagers really that good at keeping secrets, or are parents just good at deluding themselves? Or do we all want to hold on to some vision of ourselves as young smart-alecky renegades, bad boys and bad girls, who weren't so nerdy that we never sneaked a cigarette, a beer, or a joint, but who were smart enough not to get caught?

Not long after the Bad Report Card from high school, that smell—the smell that drove us nuts when Taz started using Axe—had returned to our house, and with it all of our old suspicions that he was smoking. What exactly he might be smoking, we weren't sure.

Of course, as usual, Taz insisted that he was innocent of all accusations. We knew that he was hanging out with a kid who did smoke, and, of course, that could explain the smell of cigarettes on Taz's clothes. We talked ad nauseam about the dangers of secondhand smoke, and we told him to tell his friend, "You can't smoke around me," for both their sakes, but we doubted that he would. And even if he did say something to the other kid, we realized it probably wouldn't do any good.

Taz also pointed out that he didn't need to hang out with this kid to be around smokers—if he wanted, he could get his own cigarettes, and pot, too, and anything else he wanted, for that matter. He said it was "all over his school, all over the neighborhood, all over the freaking world, and you're living in a dream if you don't think so."

I mentioned the names of a couple of kids his age who I was sure didn't smoke, who I was sure were perfect role models. "They're not tempted by all these bad things," I said.

He looked at me and grinned.

"What, what's the grin for?" I said.

"I'll never tell," he said, and walked away, suggesting, without saying as much, that even the kids who seemed perfect had their secrets.

But that crazy smell kept haunting us, and when he wasn't blaming his friend's cigarettes, he blamed eau de Axe. Finally, in a fit one day, I threw away all the Axe. He had quite a collection in there—three or four cans. I told him he could use the Ban Roll-On like me and his father.

And then I set out to discover if I really was living in a dream world. Am I hopelessly naive, or is every teenager in the world really doing bad things in secret, and none of us is willing to acknowledge reality?

My friend Barbara, a perfectly upstanding suburban mother whose daughter has been shuttled in a large air-conditioned SUV from lesson to lesson from the time she was two, often laughs about the sex and drug adventures she had in high school. But she's certain her teenage daughter is chaste.

"How do you know?" I asked.

"I just know," she said. "I can tell."

Which reminded me of when I was in high school and my best friend Susan and I were trying to figure out which girls were still virgins and which weren't.

"They walk different afterward," Susan assured me. "You can always tell."

Well, I tried to figure it out just by watching people walk down the hallway at school, but honestly, all I could tell was that some girls had big butts and some didn't.

Then there are all the people I know who spent half their teenage years stoned. One friend from when I was a kid, Cindy, wasn't exactly hiding it—the red eyes, the smell. She was so addicted that once she tried to give pot up for twenty-four hours on a bet and couldn't.

I sometimes imagine calling Cindy's mother up and saying, "How could you not have known what a pothead Cindy was?"

But maybe she did know. Maybe she just didn't know what to say.

But while some mothers deny the possibility that their kids could be doing all the bad things they did when they were teenagers, others say the opposite.

"They all do it," one mom told me matter-of-factly. Her son was a few years older than Taz, and he'd admitted to her that he and his friends do occasionally smoke pot. She told me she smoked when she was a teenager but eventually stopped.

"But what about the ones who don't stop?" I said.

"My opinion?" she said. "They're self-medicating. They have other problems, and they're smoking because they can't deal with their lives."

Did Taz need to self-medicate? I decided to find out.

"Taz," I said one day when the time seemed right, "is something bothering you?"

He was listening to his iPod, writing on his Facebook page on his laptop, had the TV on in front of him, and also had the house phone and his cell phone nearby just in case he needed more stimulation. Not surprisingly, he hadn't heard a word I said.

"Huh?" he said when he realized I was trying to get his attention.

"Is there anything we need to talk about? Any problems you might have? Because you know that Dad and I are here to listen. And if it's something serious, or something you don't want to tell us, you have an aunt who loves you, too."

He looked at me like I was out of my mind. "What are you talking about?"

"I just want to make sure that you're not smoking because you're, I don't know, depressed, or worried, or you think you have to smoke to be cool or something."

"Mom, I told you, I don't smoke!"

"OK, just checking!" I said cheerily. "Just making sure you're not, you know, self-medicating!"

He gave me another one of those "I have no idea what you're saying" looks, shook his head, mumbled, "Whatever," and went back to the computer.

It's strange comparing my attitudes about all this to my parents'. Both of them smoked several packs of nonfilter cigarettes a day, and I don't remember either of them ever lecturing me about cigarettes. Smoking was so widely accepted when I was a little girl that if you ask anyone my age what they made in kindergarten as presents for Mother's and Father's Days, a significant proportion will rightly recall making ashtrays out of modeling clay.

Yes, ashtrays were a de rigueur item in every household then. Even if your parents didn't smoke, they needed ashtrays in the living room for when company came, and it was considered perfectly appropriate to have five- and six-year-olds making these items in school to bring home as gifts. Sure, we made pot holders from those little colored loops, and yarn-embossed picture frames, too, but it's the ashtray concept that seems mind-boggling now. If you told this to kids nowadays, they'd never believe you.

And, by the way, in a lot of schools and day care centers nowadays, they've given up the concept of celebrating Mother's and Father's Days altogether. There are so many kids being raised by single parents, grandparents, gay parents, foster parents, and other unconventional households, that acknowledging Mother's and Father's Days makes some kids feel left out and sad. So some schools have banned both holidays.

I just hope that every kid has someone in this world who's crazy about them, whether it's a mother, a father, a grandparent, a second cousin twice removed, or even just the dog. Maybe schools that are worried about hurt feelings on Mother's and Father's Days could just substitute a random day and call it Someone Who Loves You Day. And instead of making ashtrays for the person, maybe six-year-olds could just sign a pledge on a drawing of a big heart that says, "I promise not to drive you crazy when I turn thirteen."

The other thing that's changed since I was a kid are the legal ramifications of smoking pot. It didn't used to be all that unusual to find people walking down the street smoking pot. You'd go to a concert in the park and the air was thick with it. When I got to college and settled in my dorm, who was living down the hall from me but a guy who was putting himself through school by selling pot. But nobody got arrested for these things.

Now we know plenty of instances of kids Taz's age getting busted for pot. The cops see them in the park, or someone at school finds out they have something on them, and the next thing you know, their parents— normal middle-class, law-abiding people who care about SAT scores and dental floss—are in court begging the judge to expunge their kids' criminal records.

The school I attended as a teenager even had a smoking bathroom for the kids. The thinking was, you can't stop kids from experimenting with cigarettes, so just contain it. It was considered a progressive concept, believe it or not, and sometimes kids would smoke pot in there, too, to which the school administration turned a blind eye. Now you couldn't even get away with a smoking bathroom for grown-ups, much less for kids.

I decided to ask my friend Linda for her take on all of this. She has no children but for some reason seems to have more common sense about raising children than any mother I know, maybe because she has nothing at stake.

Or maybe it's because of the jobs she's had. She's been a professor and she's worked at a zoo. Dealing with college students and wild animals is probably not that different from dealing with adolescents.

She herself doesn't smoke pot, but she told me she thought that "probably there is nothing really wrong with smoking pot except that it's illegal. But no one trusts adolescents to deal with nuance, I guess."

She pointed out, and rightly so, that "the illegal part should be enough by itself—I mean, isn't 'don't do illegal stuff' a pretty straightforward thing to demand of your offspring? You don't feel the need to justify why stealing or any number of other things are illegal, right?"

She added that it should be a given that kids are not allowed to break the law—at least while you are still providing food and shelter to them—no matter what people think of the particular law in question.

For the record, I smoked pot maybe a couple of times (though I was older than Taz). Looking back on it, let me just say it was mostly a waste of time, hanging out with moronic people doing idiotic things. And PS: My mother definitely never, ever knew.

Well, OK: Maybe she knew one time, after I'd spent the weekend at a friend's house when, you guessed it, her parents were away. I came home, and, well, let's just say that I was not in good shape.

But my mother never said anything to me about it. Instead, she called my sister, who was older and no longer living at home. My sister refused to confirm my mother's suspicions, and my mother was too chicken, or too befuddled, to mention it directly to me.

But now that I'm the mother, see, it's different.

I mean, I completely understand the need for both parties to deny and obfuscate. It's a natural reaction. From the kid's point of view, not only do you not want to get in trouble, but you also actually think you're doing the parents a favor by protecting them from something they wish with all their hearts wasn't so. It's a strange sort of reverse paternalism.

When they're little, we try not to talk about the fact that the dog won't live forever. And when they get big, they try not to let the parents realize that all the effort we've put into child rearing has basically been a failure. They hide, as best they can, the fact that they're breaking all the rules we set; they're trying to save us from disappointment.

That—and they don't want to get grounded for the rest of the decade, have their allowance stopped, and their cell phone contract cancelled.

There were a few times in high school when my parents went away. They left money for pizza and said I could have a slumber party so that I wouldn't be lonely. (I have to pause here for a minute to underscore the naïveté of parents who leave a teenager alone for the weekend, and their big concern is that their kid might be *lonely!*)

Of course, I immediately went down to the corner liquor store with the pizza money and bought gin. The drinking age then was only eighteen, so it wasn't such a big deal to sell alcohol to teenagers. Then my friends came over for the slumber party, and we all got drunk.

One of my parents' only worries about the sleepover was that we might stay up all night and not be rested enough for school on Monday.

You'll be relieved to hear that we did not stay up all night. We just drank until we passed out, one by one.

Fortunately, I didn't really know any boys to invite, going to an all-girl school, so there was only so much trouble we could get into. Throwing up in the toilet after drinking too much gin mixed with Hawaiian Punch was about the worst of it, and while cleaning up the resulting mess wasn't a lot of fun, especially with a hangover, it was the least I could do to keep my parents from having a nervous breakdown when they got back.

Foolishly, I somehow thought that my own youthful transgressions would make it easier for me once I was the mother of a teenager. I figured parents of my generation couldn't be shocked at anything our kids did. After all, there wasn't a whole lot we hadn't already seen or done ourselves.

Now I see how naive I was to think that. It's true that I'm not easily offended; I use plenty of four-letter words, I lived with my spouse for years before we were married, and I went to Grateful Dead concerts with the best of 'em. I am neither an old-fashioned pill with outmoded standards nor a control freak.

But in some ways it's even worse for me than it was for my mother. She had no idea what went on at concerts. But I do! She had no idea what went on at frat parties. But I do! And she had no idea what went on in people's homes when parents were away. But I do! And even though I understand at some level that teenagers have to break some rules to grow up, I realize now that parents have to make the rules anyway.

I've always hated the policeman part of being a mother. I much preferred the part where you decorated cupcakes and taught them how to doggie paddle. But those skills are irrelevant by the time your kid is thirteen. I never saw myself as one of those überneurotic controlling mothers, but how can I remain calm or be OK about any behavior that suggests my son might be headed for delinquency? The stakes are way too high.

When my kids were babies and then toddlers and then preschoolers, caring for them was physically exhausting and frequently mind-numbing. "It gets easier," said a friend whose son was much older. "And then it gets harder." Now I know what she means. I'm not up at 2 a.m. soothing a screaming infant, but I have had fights at midnight with a kid who's as tall as I am about turning off the computer, the cell phone, and the television. And I can definitely keep myself awake for hours worrying about what kind of decisions Taz will make when I'm not there to scold or shame him into doing the right thing.

Every few months on the ordinarily sedate block where I live now, a Saturday night will explode with raucous laughter, shouts, and a gaggle of teenagers staggering down the street. They'll pound on parked cars, make out under streetlamps, upend garbage cans, throw up in the gutter, and sometimes engage in a fistfight or two.

The first time this happened, shortly after we'd moved to the area, I had no idea what was going on. I was so worried that I actually asked one of my neighbors whether we should be calling 911. I didn't know if it was an incipient riot out there or what. My neighbor explained that one of the families on the block had a country house that they went to, and sometimes their teenager stayed home while the parents were gone and had some friends over.

"Oh, I get it," I said. "No need to call the cops in that case."

Indeed, I could only imagine the parents' preparations: money left for takeout, emergency phone numbers, reminders to walk the dog and take in the paper, don't leave the windows open if you go out, and sure, invite a couple of friends over to watch a movie.

Ha! You'd think none of these parents had ever been teenagers. Even if they were so nerdy that they never pulled a trick like this when they were kids, haven't they ever seen *Risky Business* or one of those TV shows where the kids throw wild parties the minute the parents drive away? That's why I've made it very clear to Taz and Sport that their father and I won't be going away for the weekend without them until they are thirty-six and thirty-one, respectively.

But I don't begin to pretend that it keeps my son out of trouble for me to sit home every night. He's off at other kids' houses, he's in the park, he's hanging out on the avenue with the pack of kids Elon and I refer to as CONY—Cream of Neighborhood Youth.

They huddle outside the local pizzeria and sit in the shadows of the elementary school playground, clouds of smoke forming overhead, the occasional loud snicker punctuating their murmured secrets. They're almost ganglike, the way they congregate and spar, bursts of "FUCK no!" and other intelligent expressions rising every now and then into the quiet night air from their huddles. One kid might break into the dance steps to "Crank That (Soulja Boy)" while another crows a few lyrics from some nasty song like "I was gonna go to schoo-ool, until I got hi-igh!" that makes the rest of them crack up.

It's a little intimidating to be an adult walking past the pack, ashamed of the jeans that I bought for twelve bucks at a closeout sale and totally unhip New Balance sneakers. But they mostly don't notice me. I'm invisible to them, and it's just as well. It allows me to discreetly observe. I fancy myself a sort of Margaret Mead, trying to figure out the coming-of-age rituals of middle-class American kids in the early twenty-first century.

I see that it's the odd one who doesn't have a cell phone, and that at least half of them are smoking cigarettes. Some boys have long hippie hair, some have buzz cuts, and some have spiky Mohawks, lohawks, faux-hawks, or frohawks—all shorter, less-in-your-face versions of the original.

(I should note here that at the tender age of nine, Sport wanted to get a Mohawk and I was dead set against it, but Elon said that maybe if we let him do it, it wouldn't seem so alluring. Well, we let him get it, and he looked like a bald guy with a squirrel on his scalp. Two weeks later, he asked to go back to the barber to have it shaved off. I had to hand it to Elon; it was a good lesson that sometimes if you can stand to let your kid do a stupid thing, he'll come to his senses faster than if you fight with him about it.)

The girls I see on the street are mostly long-haired, and most of them manage to show cleavage. I didn't even know I had cleavage until I was pregnant and spilling out of my clothes unintentionally, but it seems to be the norm now, thanks to bras that squish your boobs together and shirts that have necklines nowhere near your neck.

Most of the teenagers I see in the neighborhood from a distance look scary, intimidating, or, in the case of girls, dressed way too sexy for my standards. But once I get up close enough, I realize I've known half of them since they were four years old and riding their tricycles around the block. It's just that now they're all taller than I am.

The ones who give me hope are the ones who actually make eye contact and say hi when they realize that the unsightly grown-up slinking past on the way to pick up a quart of milk on a Saturday night is actually the mother of their old friend Taz from second grade.

The ones who frighten me are the ones who glance at me long enough to recognize me but who don't dare acknowledge that they know me, for fear of appearing uncool in front of their peers.

But these days you don't have to actually see teenagers in the flesh to observe their ways. I know more than one mother who uses the Internet to keep tabs (also known as spying) and even entrap. One friend of mine hacks into her son's e-mail to read the exchanges between him and his girlfriend. So far she hasn't found anything that's required intervention, but I wonder what she would do if she did.

Another friend took on a fake identity, created a MySpace page and an IM name, and tried to make friends with her own daughter online, just to see what she was up to.

Smart kid; she never responded.

But I have to wonder: Was the girl really avoiding strangers?

Or had she somehow figured out that her mother *was* the stranger?

# GETTING TO KNOW YOU

*I* know a lot of old-timers say it was better when parents didn't get down on the floor and play with their children, but, for the most part, I actually enjoyed playing with my boys when they were little. For me, being a mother was a way of reliving some of the fun things from my own childhood.

I got to read them all my favorite children's books, like *Eloise* and *One Morning in Maine* and *Curious George* and *Caps for Sale*. I got to play Red Light, Green Light, One, Two, Three and Giant Step. And I got to go to all my favorite places—parks, zoos, the circus, country fairs—and enjoy them all over again in the company of my kids.

I loved doing arts and crafts, too, though my boys got sick of Play-Doh and painting with glitter long before I did. I also got to play with all the toys that I didn't have when I was a child—like Erector sets, trains, and cars, which weren't considered suitable toys for little girls way back in the last century, but which are really a lot of fun.

When the boys outgrew toys, we moved on to games. I didn't play many board games when I was a child, but as a mother, I learned Trouble, Sorry!, Scrabble, and Stratego—and I even won sometimes. The kids tried to teach me chess, but I proved too stupid to learn it. We've played a lot of Monopoly over the years, too, though I don't love it—the games just go on too long—but I am always happy to engage in a gin rummy marathon.

Part of the shock of having a teenager, though, is that all of a sudden your kid doesn't want to play games with you anymore. He doesn't want to go places and do things with you, or even be seen with you.

On the one hand, I understand that it's normal for kids to push their parents away as they grow up. On the other hand, I wasn't willing to accept being cut off this way from my own son just because he had turned thirteen. I actually missed spending time with Taz. I was starting to feel like I didn't know who he was. One day I realized I couldn't even remember the last time we'd done something simple and fun together.

I decided we needed some mother-son quality time. I offered to take him to the beach, the pool, the bowling alley, the mall. I'd play cards, or even the dreaded Monopoly. How about a bike ride, or maybe a jog in the park?

"Nah, that's OK," he'd say, no matter what I offered to do. "I got some people I gotta hang out with today."

I sometimes heard other parents describe what sounded like idyllic family outings to museums, historic sites, and other attractions. It made me wonder what was wrong with me that I couldn't get Taz to go places with me.

Then, one day, I dropped in on a friend who'd recently renovated her home. She wanted me to see the new cabinets, tiles, and paint colors. But when I got there, I witnessed firsthand just what these allegedly idyllic family outings I've been jealous of are really all about.

It was 11 a.m. on a Sunday and her thirteen-year-old had just been awakened by his little sister. He was not happy about it, because, apparently, he believed he was entitled to sleep all day.

Not so, said his mother. They were heading out to a museum to see a spectacular exhibit about the evolution of modern architecture, and she wanted to leave within twenty minutes. It was a beautiful day, so they were also going to be picnicking in a park en route. She had a lovely basket all prepared, with his favorite ham-and-cheese sandwiches. As a special treat for him, she had even gone to the trouble of purchasing sour cream and onion potato chips.

Well, all that might work on an eight-year-old, but, apparently, it wasn't enough to get an adolescent out of bed on a Sunday morning.

"I'm not hungry," he moaned. "I don't care. I just want to sleep."

"Well, that's not happening," said the mother matter-of-factly. "You need to get up, brush your teeth, and get dressed so that we can go."

"I'm not GOING!" the kid screamed. "I TOLD you, I don't WANT to go!"

"Well, it's NOT UP TO YOU!" the mother screamed back. "This is what we're doing today, and YOU'RE coming whether you like it or NOT!"

"I HATE you!" came the response. "I hate EVERYONE in this FAMILY!"

I fervently wished at that moment that I could have shrunk myself to the size of a dust ball (not that she had any, her house seemed spotless) and rolled away on the still-glossy, just-polyurethaned wood floors to hide under the tastefully reupholstered sofa. Should I have just turned around and let myself out, or would that have been too rude? On the other hand, I didn't exactly want to interfere in this little conflagration to bid my good-byes. I didn't want to further embarrass my friend by reminding her that she had a witness to this outburst, but I also didn't have the slightest bit of curiosity about how it was going to turn out. I'd been there, I really had, and the endings to these episodes were never pretty.

At some point in the argument, she sighed and turned to me, bit her lip, and shook her head.

"I sympathize with you," I said. "I really do. We have the exact same thing happening in our house all the time. Speaking of which, I'm gonna run. Good luck! See ya."

I turned tail and dashed out the door, and realized, somewhat guiltily, that actually we hadn't had this same exact problem in our house lately, because when Taz said no, he didn't want to do something, I never argued. I guess this makes me a wimp. Or maybe just a Terrible Mother.

As further evidence that my own child was becoming a stranger to me, one day another mother told me that the photo on Taz's Facebook page was a good one.

I was embarrassed to admit that I had no idea what she was talking about. Terrible Mother that I am, I had not kept tabs on my son's Facebook page; I wasn't even sure what a Facebook page was. Turned out my friend's son had a Facebook page, too, and my son was a Facebook friend of her son's, so that's how she knew about the photo on Taz's page.

Not that I understood any of this. Clearly, I needed to get on board with this Facebook thing. So I went to the Facebook website and supplied my e-mail address to register.

Moments later, I got a message informing me that I had just invited forty-three people to be my Facebook friends! Some of them were people I hadn't heard from in years, including assorted cousins, high school classmates I hadn't kept in touch with, and others from various phases of my life, like a student from a college class I taught four years earlier and a political consultant I had once quoted for a news story I wrote during the 2000 election campaign.

I wasn't sure what I'd clicked or done to get this list

of people, but the whole thing was mortifying. People I hadn't spoken to in eight years were getting invitations to be my Facebook friend? How embarrassing!

Suddenly, e-mails started popping up in my in-box. A couple of relatives were the first to respond. Yes, they did want to be my Facebook friends. Hurray! I was touched by this, and pleased. Then I reminded myself not to get too carried away—these people were my cousins, after all. If they won't be my Facebook friends, who will?

But as the minutes wore on, I wondered why so few of the rest of the forty-three invitees were responding. Had they gotten the invitation and thought, "UGH! I don't want HER to be my Facebook friend!" Or were they simply wondering, "Who the hell is this?" since they hadn't heard from me in years and quite possibly had forgotten who I was. I was starting to feel paranoid, and not a little bit depressed.

Then I got another e-mail from someone wanting to be my Facebook friend, only it was someone whose name was utterly unknown to me. I was certain this person was not on my original list of potential Facebook friends. I went to his Facebook page to check him out, and he definitely did not look familiar. His profile described him as a graduate student from Wyoming. I wracked my brain. Did I know this person? How could this person know me? It was all maddening, like something out of *Minority Report* or *The Matrix*. Maybe I knew him in my OTHER life, with my OTHER brain?

It was like my e-mail address was living some secret life without me, just like when I tie my dog up outside a store to run a quick errand, and I come out and people I don't know are talking to the dog by name. "Hi, Buddy! How are you?" some strange guy is crooning at her. I mean, excuse me, but how the hell does my dog have human friends whom I don't know? When I'm brave enough to ask, there's always some logical explanation—"Oh, I work at the dog boarding place, and I remember the time Buddy stayed with us for a few days," or something like that—but it's still rather disorienting to think that your pet knows more people in the neighborhood than you do.

This Facebook thing was a little bit like that. I wanted to e-mail this guy and say, "But who are you? Why do you want to be my Facebook friend when I've never heard of you?" But I was too embarrassed. I mean, what if I did know him, somehow, through work, or some class I'd taken long ago or something, and I just didn't remember. Or maybe he was one of those Internet stalkers the FBI is always busting, and he somehow thinks I'm a teenager from Alabama who will meet him at a bus station, instead of a forty-something mother of two who has a lot of bad hair days.

I reminded myself that I'd started out on Facebook just wanting to see my own son's photo, but now, somehow, I was spending all this time obsessing over who was and wasn't friending me.

So I forced myself to get to the task at hand and look

for Taz's page. I found it easily enough. On it was a photo of him with a girl I didn't recognize. She had her arms wrapped around him and an expression of utter glee on her face. But he was staring straight at the camera, looking positively bored. There was nothing salacious about it, and yet his look of "been there, done that" ennui was somehow a little disturbing.

A day or so later, Taz checked his Facebook account and saw that there was an invitation from me wanting to be his Facebook friend. Even more horrifying, he realized that many other people he knew had gotten an invitation from his mother to be their Facebook friends.

Meanwhile, I still hadn't quite figured out how to have my own Facebook page, or what I would do with a Facebook page about myself if I could figure out how to make one, but one bright spot was that I already had a Facebook invitation to do lunch with one of my cousins.

"Why did you go on Facebook?" Taz demanded.

"I wanted to see your page," I said. "Mike's mom said your picture was really good."

"You shouldn't have gone on there. Don't you know how embarrassing this is? Facebook is for teenagers!"

"But there's lots of moms on Facebook. I invited a whole bunch of people to be my Facebook friends, and all the ones who are my age said yes."

"Exactly! All the ones who are your age, and nobody else. You don't need Facebook. You can just make a phone call or send an e-mail or something. You need to delete your Facebook account."

"How can I delete my Facebook account when I'm not even sure how I created it?"

"Mom, please, this is humiliating!"

Finally, I agreed that now that I had achieved my objective of seeing his Facebook page, I didn't really need a Facebook page of my own. I gave him my password and told him he could delete it if he wanted to.

"Me? Why should I do it?" he said. "I'm busy!"

Well, yes, I explained to Taz, that is part of the problem—you are always busy. Even too busy to hang out with your mother, which is why I felt the need to try to get to know you through your Facebook account.

Taz never did delete my Facebook account. And neither did I. And, eventually, a funny thing happened. I became addicted to Facebook, and it had nothing to do with Taz. I think it started when a former coworker whom I hadn't heard from in years found me on Facebook and said he liked the poem I'd put on my Facebook Wall. Until that moment, I hadn't even realized other people could see my Facebook Wall. I thought it was more like a diary.

Then the lightbulb went off. It *is* a diary. But it's a *public* diary. And that's what's fun about it. (Fun, that is, as long as your father isn't running for president and your Facebook page doesn't say you support some *other* guy.) Facebook is like TV—only every single show, every minute of every single day, is about someone who's your friend.

An important breakthrough in my Facebook evolution was when my niece—the twenty-five-year-old Glam Queen of Long Island—requested me as a Facebook friend. After my experience with my son's rejection, I hadn't even bothered to ask my niece to be my Facebook friend, so I was pleased and flattered when the request came from her. She said she couldn't believe how many Facebook friends I had, and that she liked my photo. She even said she wanted to come hang out at an event I had mentioned on my Wall—an art show hosted by a friend.

This was especially amusing because my sister had just told me she didn't know if my niece was coming to the art show. She'd e-mailed and phoned her but hadn't gotten any response.

"She's definitely coming to the art show," I told my sister. "She just wrote me a note about it on my Facebook Wall."

"She wrote on your Facebook Wall?" my sister said. Then, after a pause: "You have a Facebook page?"

Suddenly, I felt so popular. It was like being back in high school—only this time I get to be one of the Cool Girls! At work, someone said that playing with Facebook was like being twenty-seven years old again. "Twenty-seven?" I said incredulously. "You mean *seventeen!*"

I now routinely waste every free minute of entire weekends on Facebook. I joined a group called "When I was your age, Pluto was a planet," and another called "People who always have to spell their names for other people." I took the movie compatibility test and was pleased to see that according to the results, my boss and I are highly compatible.

I was afraid to add the "What kind of drunk are you?" application, but I would really like to, because a woman in Denmark whom I met once for ten minutes, and who is now my Facebook friend, has it on *her* FB page. I did take the "Which Beatle are you?" quiz, and was surprised to find that I am George. (I was so sure I was John!)

Then I got my sister to sign up for Facebook, and she took a quiz to find out what type of animal she was in a past life. She was a platypus, and she talked me into taking the same quiz, and it turns out I was a platypus, too. I found this a little embarrassing, like I was being a copycat of my big sister, but, in her wise way, she assured me it was fine. "It is as it should be," she declared on her Facebook Wall. "You are my baby sister platypus."

But I didn't realize the extent of my FB addiction until 12:43 a.m. one Saturday, when I sent a message through Facebook to a friend in Seattle, where it was only 9:43 p.m. I told her how much I liked the pictures of her puppy that she had put up on her Facebook page, and she immediately wrote back, "I can't believe you're on Facebook at 12:43 a.m.! ADDICT! ADDICT!"

Facebook even started to creep into my work life. My employer has offices all over the world, and I've dealt with many colleagues by phone and e-mail without ever meeting them. Friending them on Facebook was a way of matching faces to names and getting to know them a little more personally. But this also meant that work conversations sometimes took place on Facebook. One day when a coworker sent me a work-related message on Facebook, I asked him to continue the conversation by phone.

"You have to help me stop!" I wrote. "I'm addicted to Facebook!"

"Help you stop?" he wrote back. "I can't help you stop—I'm an enabler!"

But why *can't* we stop? Well, it's just that it's so much fun. I can't wait to see what's on the little "News Feed" that tells me Ted is catching up on his reading! Diane is going to a party! Hilary just bought a car and got a job waitressing in New Zealand! I love posting my own news on my Wall—things like "I made a festive holiday craft today—I glued glitter on pinecones!"

At the same time, it was sort of horrifying that I felt the need to share the news about my festive holiday craft with my 129 FB friends (and counting). What was happening to me? I was becoming a different person, a Person Who Lives for Facebook. (This realization even prompted me to change my Facebook profile. Where it asks you to fill in religion, I wrote, "I worship Facebook." Which led one of my Facebook friends to comment, "I like your religion.")

Every few days now, I get a message from another mother who sounds just like I was when I started out on Facebook, back in the dark ages.

"Hi, I'm not sure how I found you on Facebook, but I did," wrote one friend recently. "I joined Facebook to see my son's page, but he refuses to approve me as a friend and now that I've found you, I'm not quite sure what to do."

"Put a photo on your profile," I e-mailed back. "Ask everyone in your address book to become your Facebook friend. Take the movie compatibility test and join the group 'When I was your age, Pluto was a planet.' And never mind your son—don't you know that grown-ups are ruining Facebook for the kids?

"By the way," I couldn't resist adding, "can you try the 'What kind of drunk are you?' application and tell me what it's like?"

As I pressed Send, I realized I had hit another milestone in my Facebook career.

I wasn't just an addict. I was an enabler.

## GOOD-BYE THIRTEEN,
## HELLO FOURTEEN,
## HELLO HOPE

**W**hen a revival of *A Chorus Line* came back to Broadway, I wondered if Taz would like it as much as I did when I was in high school. I'd been obsessed with the show as a teenager, and so had all my friends. Balcony tickets were just $6 when it opened in 1975, and even though I earned only a dollar an hour babysitting, at those prices I was able to see the show three times.

Thirty years later, our tickets cost $110 each, and they weren't even in the orchestra. That's our family theater allowance for the year, so I sure hoped the show would live up to my memories.

The concept of *A Chorus Line* is simple. A line of young dancers takes the stage, and one by one they tell stories of growing up and surviving the torments of adolescence in order to pursue their dreams. I remembered how meaningful it was for me to hear these tales of emerging sexuality, of trying to fit in, and of worrying if you're pretty enough or talented enough, when I myself was going through those same awkward phases.

But even as an adult, the show still resonated with me. I still knew every word of every song, and every nuance in the melodies. I cried and laughed as the dancers told their tales, and I realized all over again why the show had meant so much to me as a kid.

There is no intermission in *A Chorus Line*. It's the rare one-act musical where you can't share your opinions midshow, so I had no idea what Taz was thinking as we sat there, and he betrayed no hint of a reaction. He clapped at the right moments, laughed when everyone else did, but was he just being polite?

When it was over, we poured into the street with the rest of the audience and got on the train without speaking much.

"So, did you like it?" I finally asked.

He nodded and smiled. "It was really good," he said. But he seemed lost in his thoughts, and it was late on a school night, so I didn't push him.

When we got home, he headed straight for the computer. I was just about to tell him that he really needed to go to bed, when I heard the familiar words from one of the show's songs coming from his room: *"Hello twelve, hello thirteen, hello love . . ."*

He was downloading the song from iTunes onto his laptop. I guess that's the twenty-first-century equivalent of buying the original cast album (which, of course, I still own).

I smiled. It had to mean that he'd liked it.

In the weeks that followed, I kept humming the song

he'd downloaded, but in my mind, I had changed the lyrics to suit what was happening in our house: *"Good-bye thirteen, hello fourteen, hello hope!"*

See, Taz was about to leave the dreaded thirteenth year behind, and I was fervently praying to the God of All Mothers that the next stage of child rearing would be less trying. And gradually, very gradually, I started to feel slightly optimistic that things would be OK.

For example, all of a sudden one day, I realized it had been awhile since he'd gotten into any serious trouble. Either he was getting better at covering things up, or he was straightening out a little.

He seemed less obnoxious lately, too. If I so much as made him a sandwich, he'd say, "Thanks, Mom, I love you!" He was too young to remember Eddie Haskell from *Leave It to Beaver* telling Mrs. Cleaver how lovely she looked, so I chose to take the good vibes at face value.

And ever since the Bad Report Card, I had only gotten one e-mail from a teacher (threatening to fail him if he didn't hand in the thirty-two homework assignments that he owed; Taz claimed they really were on the floor of his room this time, and that he'd be sure to straighten it all out).

In fairness, there did seem to be a fair amount of homework being done in his room on a regular basis. I knew this because I was sometimes summoned to help explain things that I barely understood, like what the hell Demien's problem was in the Hermann Hesse novel

(I tried to read a few chapters in the hopes of figuring it out, but, frankly, could not get through it) and how you say "My dog is very intelligent" in Spanish (that one I knew), and what unilateral disengagement is (no, it has nothing to do with sex ed; it's related to peace negotiations with Israel).

He knew better than to ask me for help with math or science, but I did help him memorize a scene from *The Glass Menagerie*, and I also provided vital assistance when he had to create a three-dimensional model of a church from colonial Mexico. (I went to the store, bought a couple of Communion cards, and told him to cut the crosses and pictures of the Virgin Mary out to decorate his cardboard box with. It looked really nice when it was done, it really did.)

Another good sign was that now when Taz got Cs or Ds on his papers, he sat down and revised them and handed them in again to try to improve the grade. And a few times, he was even up very late past midnight trying to finish something due the next day.

I'd lecture him about the importance of not waiting until the last minute to complete a big project, and then I'd usually tell him it probably wasn't worth staying up all night, that he might as well just get some sleep and hand it in a day late, but he was having none of that.

"No!" he'd whine. "You don't understand! I can't do that."

There was always some reason why he had to finish it

no matter how long he stayed up, whether it was part of a team project and he didn't want to let the other person down, or because the teacher in that particular course didn't accept late work.

I had to admire his willingness to get the work done. I just wished he wasn't such a procrastinator.

One day after school, he stopped by my office. I introduced him to the book review editor, and then, remembering his famous MySpace declaration, "I hate books," I jokingly added: "But Taz hates books, so I guess there's not a lot for you two to discuss."

"I don't hate books!" Taz said in an outraged tone.

"You don't?" I said, genuinely surprised.

"No!" he replied, as if I'd insulted some deeply held value of his.

"Well, what's your favorite book?" said the editor genially, trying to help smooth out one of those awkward public tiffs between mother and son.

"Um, I think probably *Angela's Ashes*," Taz said matter-of-factly. "That was a good one."

It was something he'd been required to read for high school. Certainly, if I had suggested he read a book about a mother raising two sons in the last century, he would have run screaming in the other direction.

"And *Catcher in the Rye*," he added as an afterthought. "That was pretty good, too."

The book editor smiled at me. "So I guess he doesn't hate books after all," he said.

"I guess not," I said.

To myself, I said: *Good-bye thirteen, hello fourteen, hello hope!*

One night I was hanging out with Sport playing Monopoly. We hadn't seen Taz all evening. He'd left a message at some point to say he wouldn't be home for dinner. Although it was hard to accept his wanderings and disappearing acts at first, by this point in my life as an Experienced Mother of a Teenager, I'd more or less gotten used to it and I'd sort of given up tracking him down, so I didn't even try to call him back. My standards had definitely declined.

Then the dog lifted her head, perked up her ears, and walked to the door expectantly.

Sport looked at me and smiled. "Taz is home," he said.

Sure enough, the door opened and slammed shut a moment later.

"Hi, Mom!"

It was indeed Taz, home from a night of . . . chillin' . . . or . . . gulp . . . who knows what. He walked into the room and handed me a twenty.

"Here's your money back," he said. "Remember you gave it to me yesterday? I didn't need it after all. I was at Ethan's house and his mom made dinner for us, so I didn't need to buy any food."

"Um, OK."

"Oh, I forgot to tell you Friday—I got an A on my history paper, the one on Buddhism."

He was grinning. When I didn't grin back, he prompted me.

"Isn't that great? I can't wait to tell Dad."

I nodded stupidly.

Maybe he didn't hate us? Maybe chillin' was more innocent than I had imagined? Maybe he was actually a good boy instead of the fiend of my nightmares? Maybe I had been right to Keep Hope Alive?

"Taz, when are we gonna go to the movies?" Sport asked. "I really wanna see the new Harry Potter."

"Um, I don't know, maybe this weekend?" Taz said "I'll check the schedule at the theater."

Then he spied a pile of clean laundry on a tabletop. "Don't worry about this, I'll put my stuff away," he said, scooping up the shirts, pants, and boxers that belong to him.

He turned back before leaving the room and added, "You want me to walk the dog?"

He whistled and Buddy's toenails skittered on the wood floor as she slipped and slid over his way, tail wagging.

"C'mon, Buddy," he said, "let's go. G'night."

"G'night," I said.

He walked down the hall. I heard him opening and shutting drawers as he put his clothes away, then the jangle of the dog's leash being snapped on her collar, and the door slamming as they went out to walk around the block.

Before they returned, Sport wiped me out with the rent on a hotel on Boardwalk. "You want to play again?" he asked hopefully.

I shook my head.

"Time for bed," I said. "Go brush your teeth. Make sure you do it for the whole two minutes now, remember what the dentist said, use the timer, OK?"

"OK," he said.

I could hear him dutifully brushing away from the kitchen as I cleaned up the Monopoly pieces.

"I love you," I called out to him, for no reason in particular.

"Love you, Mom," he said through a mouthful of toothpaste suds.

It's true that I had finally gotten used to the idea of having a teenager in the house, but I still felt so glad that my little boy was only nine.

Taz turned fourteen not long after that. But somehow it just didn't seem like that big of a deal. We didn't even have a real party. A couple of kids came over (including a girl with really nice sneakers, but I stifled the impulse to compliment her) and had a slice of pizza at our house, then they all went off to a movie. It was pretty low-key.

Did we even get Taz a present? I can't remember. But presents for kids just aren't what they used to be anyway. Half the kids I know can't even think of what they want for Christmas because they already have everything. And if they do want something, it's an iPhone or a

Wii or some other thing so expensive you have to get a second job to pay for it.

I also just found myself feeling much calmer about the concept of fourteen than I had been about the concept of thirteen. When Taz was twelve becoming a teenager, it was different. It felt momentous, and it was. I was totally unprepared for all the changes in his appearance and his behavior. But by now, I had spent so much time being appalled by everything from cigarette smoke to condoms to liquor that I almost couldn't imagine what there was left to horrify me.

Well, I guess I hadn't had to bail Taz out of the city jail yet, although prom night was a close second, and I hadn't yet found pot plants in the windowbox (though if you had told me that there was one growing in there, I suppose I wouldn't have been all that surprised). It was like I'd survived one of those military campaigns the Pentagon comes up with weird names for: Shock and Awe! Operation Rolling Thunder! The war was still going on, but now that the invasion was a distant memory, I had gotten used to bombs falling on my village every day.

Still, it never ceased to amaze me that just when I would get rid of one worry, another would come along and take its place. When Taz was twelve and wanted to go to the movies, I worried that the people in the box office wouldn't believe he still deserved the child's ticket price. When he was thirteen and going to the movies without me, I worried he'd try to sneak in as a twelve-year-old and

pay the discount price, and that just didn't seem right.
Now that he was fourteen, I worried he'd pass for seventeen and get into all the R-rated movies. My worry list was
like a treadmill.

My attitude evolved about other things, too. One
night I was on the phone with a friend who lived in the
suburbs and Taz was heading out the door. I interrupted
my conversation to give him the usual third degree:
Where are you going? Who are you going with? When
are you coming home? Be careful, don't get in trouble.
How are you getting there?

Turned out he was taking the train to a friend's house
in another neighborhood, and I was actually feeling just
a little bit proud, as my friend overheard snatches of the
conversation, of how independent Taz was. This was
partly why I had decided it was a good thing to raise my
children in the city, because they wouldn't need to be
chauffeured everywhere by their parents, and they also
wouldn't be driving each other around as teenagers.

When I got back on the phone, though, my friend
said that after listening to my conversation with Taz,
she was so glad she lived in a place where kids need to be
driven everywhere.

"Why?" I asked.

"Because you just have a lot more control that way."

I realized she was right. Taz would be gone for hours,
and I would just have to take his word for it if he called
me, saying he was at so-and-so's house. If I'd driven him
to his friend's house, I'd know for sure that's where he

was. I might see his friend, get a read on what was happening there, even say hi to the parents.

As it was now, I couldn't even be sure there were any parents over there. I suddenly realized that the good thing about being forced to drive kids everywhere is that every time they change locations, some grown-up gets to step in and assess the situation. Maybe if you know somebody's dad is going to be looking into your eyes in an hour or sitting next to you, you'll be more careful about whether your breath smells like booze or your clothes reek of smoke.

Of course, what's bad about living someplace where kids have to be driven everywhere is that all those kids eventually turn sixteen and learn to drive themselves. And as some of my friends who grew up in suburbs have told me, there's nothing to stop your kid from finding another kid who lives within walking distance and whose parents are gone, at which point your kid has a new place to commit all his evil deeds.

But at that moment, on the phone with my friend, the idea of reducing some of the independence that I had once thought of as positive seemed appealing.

And yet I also knew it was too late to curb Taz's wanderings. I grew up in the city, too. I remembered how thrilling it was to take the train to visit friends in places I'd never been because I suddenly had friends in high school who didn't live within walking distance of my house. I felt so grown-up figuring out how to get to the Bronx by myself to hang out with a friend on a Saturday, or to distant Queens for a party. I wondered if my mother had worried about me the way I worried about Taz. I suppose she had, but if she did, I don't remember her admitting it.

And yet, in a weird way, I sort of admired Taz's mastery of the trains and buses. He'd surpassed me in that regard. One day Taz told me he was going to Sea Gate to visit a friend, a neighborhood I had only vaguely heard of. I felt a pride only a city mom can have as I listened to him explain the web of trains and buses he'd be taking to get there.

One Saturday night, Taz told me he was taking the bus with some friends to sleep over at one of their houses—one of those houses where there was plenty of room for a couple of big guys to stretch out, and a really nice dad who more often than not could be persuaded to take them all to a diner for breakfast Sunday morning. I knew the other two boys he was going with, and it all sounded perfectly fine. It was around 9:30 p.m. when Taz left, and I was tired. I had learned long ago that I need more sleep than my children, and that there's no shame in saying that it's my bed time, even if it's not theirs. I told Elon and Sport good night, and I turned in.

I was awakened some time later by some sort of commotion. I heard Taz's voice. What was he doing home? Didn't he say he was going to sleep over at his buddy's house?

I tried to figure out what was happening by listening

to the voices in the hallway, but it didn't quite make sense to me, so I turned the light on and got out of bed.

I saw Taz and I wanted to cry. The skin around his left eye was swollen, purple and blue.

"What happened?" I said.

"We were getting out of the bus and these guys jumped us," he said quietly.

Taz had gotten away from the attackers and had run to get his friend's dad, who lived just around the corner, but the bad guys ran off after giving them each a slug. They didn't steal anything—not that a couple of fourteen-year-olds have much worth stealing. Seemed like they were in it only for the thrill.

The father called an ambulance, and the paramedics said the kids were all basically OK. The cops said each boy would have to come to the precinct with a parent if we wanted to make a report, but Taz said that seemed pointless.

"You could have called us," I said. "We would have come and picked you up."

"I didn't want to upset you," he said. "I figured it was just better to come back here." The other boy's dad had driven him home.

I was trying hard not to smother Taz with sympathy or make it out to be worse than it was. I offered him an ice pack and a Tylenol, and told him that nobody lived in New York without eventually becoming a crime victim. It wasn't like he'd done anything wrong; he'd been taking the bus, for God's sake, from one safe neighborhood to another safe neighborhood. It wasn't even that late—before 10 p.m. He hadn't been alone, and goodness knows, if I'd been looking to mug somebody, those three big boys certainly didn't look like easy targets to me.

But then who knows what motivates a couple of bad boys to beat someone up. If they'd wanted an easy mark, surely there was a little old lady getting off that bus, too. Maybe what they prized was the challenge of picking on another teenager. Maybe Taz was big enough now to count as a conquest. Maybe because my kid had a black eye, somebody else's kid had passed an initiation rite into some evil gang somewhere.

Back when I was trying to navigate the Land of Thirteen-Year-Olds, things frequently seemed absurd, unfathomable, incomprehensible. Things were darker on Planet Fourteen, but in some ways they were more recognizable to a grown-up. Forget about the "Whassup, JC" prattle of last year. The right response to what happened to Taz that night was OMG WTF.

On the other hand, I tried to put it in perspective, both for me and for Taz.

"Listen," I said, "when you're older, you'll get called for jury duty. And there's always this moment in the courtroom when the judge asks whether anybody in the jury pool has ever been a victim of a crime."

"Why do they need to know that?"

"Well, they want to see if you can be fair when you hear the evidence. If you've been robbed, then maybe you can't be objective listening to a case about a robbery. So the DA and the defense attorney need to know what everyone's experience has been with the criminal justice system."

"Your point is?"

"Well, it's just that when they ask if anyone's been a victim of a crime, I've never been in a jury pool where everyone didn't raise their hand. So my point is just that most people at some point end up having a run-in with a bad guy. It might be something simple—your car got broken into, your wallet got lifted from your purse. But you just hope you don't get hurt. And you weren't seriously hurt, thank goodness. So maybe this was the one thing that had to happen to you so that you can be one with your fellow jurors and raise your hand when they ask that question. It might be the only good thing about what happened tonight."

Taz let out a chuckle and nodded. He got what I was saying.

"You gonna be able to go to sleep?" I asked.

"Yeah, don't worry about it," he said. "I'm OK."

"All right," I said. "If you wake up in the night, and you're freaking out, or whatever, you're allowed to wake me up. OK?"

"OK."

But I knew he'd never do that, and he didn't.

When they're little, and you go for years without a good night's sleep, you wonder if they'll ever make it through to morning without finding some reason to wake you up. But then one day you look at the clock and it's 7:30 a.m., and you realize that nobody called for you in the dark, nobody crawled in your bed and stuck their frozen toes on your warm knees.

For a panicked moment, you wonder if your child is—well, I can't even say it. You leap out of bed and run into his room and if you haven't wakened him up with all your commotion by then, you stand there for a minute trying to make sure that he's still breathing. You see the chest rising and falling and you let out a sigh. There's nothing wrong. He's just growing up. He doesn't need you anymore, is all; he doesn't need to wake you up in the night.

Taz was pretty good about calling me after school most days to let me know his schedule, but one day I didn't hear from him. I didn't get too worried, though; it was no longer that unusual for him to occasionally go missing for a while. Finally, he came through the door around 6 p.m., looking both exhausted and triumphant.

"Where were you?" I asked.

"Coney Island," he said.

It was the dead of winter, so I knew he hadn't been at the beach or the amusement park.

"Why?"

"By accident, I forgot my backpack on the train with all my books and my homework in it, and when I asked the worker in the station for help, he said the only way to get it back was to go to the end of the line, to the depot at Coney Island."

He then told me a long, complicated story in which he took the next train all the way out to Coney Island, about a half hour from our house, and pretty much got the runaround—as you might expect—from every person he asked for help in recovering the lost backpack.

But he was just determined to get it back, and basically went from worker to worker at the depot until he located the one who remembered removing his backpack when the train was cleaned at the end of the line. That worker then took him to the room where they kept lost property, and there, indeed, was the missing bag, with all his schoolwork in it.

"You should have called me!" I said. "I would have driven you out there. I would have gone with you. I would have helped you look for it."

He shrugged. "It's OK," he said. "I figured it out."

I was impressed. And I also realized that had he called me for help instead of trying to figure it out himself, I might have told him not to bother going to the depot. I have never heard of anyone losing anything on the train and finding it again, and I tend to wither in the face of bureaucracies. It was just as well he'd decided to handle it on his own; my pessimism would have been more of a liability than a help.

I was proud of him for solving his own problem that day. And I took a step back and considered it all. If Taz could lose his backpack on the subway and then find it again without my help, and if he could get socked in the eye and not feel the need to call home right away, well, maybe that was a good thing.

Maybe it meant I had done my job as a mother, and raised him right.

Or maybe it just meant he was old enough now to realize that there was nothing I could do to make it better.

Whichever it was, one thing was for sure: My unjumpable son was no longer unjumpable.

## MEDITATIONS ON
## THE PAST AND FUTURE

**B**y the time Taz turned fourteen, my life had revolved around my children for so many years—and happily so, for the most part, entertainingly so—that I couldn't imagine what it would be like when they were grown up and gone.

I can no longer even remember what I did in my spare time before I had children, and that's probably proof that whatever it was, it wasn't very important. Oh, I suppose before I had kids, I ate out more, and saw more foreign films, and maybe I went to grown-up parties, but I actually don't recall any of that as being more interesting than watching a baby learn to walk and talk.

I'm not saying that every aspect of child rearing is fascinating. I remember going to the playground at a time when I had probably gone to the playground at least once a day for eight years straight. (When your kids are five years apart in age, early childhood lasts a very long time.) But when I plopped myself down on the park bench, I was immediately overcome with the need to sleep.

I actually thought I was going to pass out. I could barely keep my eyes open, and I kept snapping my head back up every time it lolled to the side. I realized I was sort of making a spectacle of myself, and tried hard to straighten myself up on the hard wooden bench in the hope that an erect posture would fool my body into thinking it wasn't time for bed.

It also wasn't the first time this had happened. Lately, it seemed like whenever I went to the playground, I felt positively narcoleptic.

Just then, a father I knew sat down next to me and said hello.

"How are you?" he said. "What's new?"

"Oh, nothing much," I said, stifling a yawn, then letting out a little laugh. "Oh my, excuse me! I didn't mean to yawn in your face! It's just the strangest thing, though. Every time I come to the playground with the kids, as soon as I get here, I feel like I'm going to fall fast asleep."

The father looked at me skeptically. "You think you're the only one?"

"What do you mean?"

"Everybody feels that way."

"They do?"

"Of course. You get here, you sit down, and it's so incredibly boring that you immediately feel like lying down to take a nap."

Leave it to a Straight-Talking Dad to set me straight on what taking a kid to the park was really all about. You can bet your yoga mat that the Perfect Mommies would never have admitted to being bored in the playground. They were too busy making sure that Other People's Babysitters weren't doing something wrong.

But as the years go by, you go to the playground less and less. At some point, you're asking the kids if they want to go there more than they're asking you to take them.

And then one day you realize it's been months since you went to the playground. Your kids have outgrown the swings and those stupid boxy climbing thingies that replaced the much more interesting (and more dangerous) monkey bars of your childhood.

Now they're playing video games with their friends, instant-messaging kids in their class and begging for a ride to the mall.

The changes can be measured in the decline of other rituals, too. There's a period of ten years or so where you have to buy your kid a new bike every other year, because he's outgrowing them so fast. Then one day you buy him an adult bike, and that's the last bike he'll ever need.

Same thing with painting the bedroom. First, you have the nursery colors, then something bright but basic. Then comes a cool and trendy look, which might just last until college starts. In Taz's case, the walls of his room are swirls of dark blue and white, evoking an ocean or a misty night sky. It's so soothing and dark, like a womb or a little boat floating in the sea.

But will I leave those blue swirls on the walls once he's off to college in a few years—a shrine to Taz's childhood? Or should I quickly paint over the ocean of blue with linen white and call it a guest room?

One day I sat down and thought about the fact that Taz was only going to be living in the house for another couple of years (please, God of All Mothers, let him get into a college that's too far away to commute to).

Maybe, I thought, I ought to try to make the place more pleasant for him in the time he had left with us. After all, when they're little, you childproof your house, and when they get bigger, you buy all kinds of stupid stuff to clutter your space with—like indoor basketball hoops and gigantic dollhouses nobody ever plays with. Maybe, I thought, there was something along those lines that a teenager might like to have in his room.

He seemed pleased when I approached him with this idea. First, he asked for cable TV, which I wasn't inclined to get. Then he asked for an air conditioner. His room was small and airless, and it did heat up like a closet in the summer.

For years, I'd taken a sort of perverse pride in knowing that my children were not so coddled they needed air-conditioning. Fans were good enough for them, I told myself! It toughens 'em up to sleep in ninety-eight-degree heat and 100 percent humidity every July! Nobody had central air when I was little; why should they have such extravagances now?

On the other hand, Elon and I had an air conditioner in our bedroom. And I recognize that the older you get, the bigger your body is, the harder it is to tolerate heat.

"OK," I promised. "I'll do it. I'll get you an AC."

The following weekend, we went and bought him an air conditioner. It was small and noisy, but it made the room ice cold in minutes.

It wasn't exactly on the level of *The Brady Bunch* episode where they created a bachelor pad for Greg, the oldest teenager. But still, Taz was grateful for it. And once it had been installed, to my surprise, he started spending more time at our house than he had in months. He was chillin' at home for a change—literally.

I have a good friend from childhood whose son is a few years older than mine. I don't see her very often, but once in a while we run into each other and chat on the avenue. I saw her not long ago, and she told me she was coming home from a piano recital.

I had no idea she played piano. She told me it was something she started doing as her son got older. Believe it or not, she told me, she had time on her hands now—time for a hobby! "You'll get there," she said. "Just wait."

I had to laugh; I'd tried studying piano when my boys were little. What was I thinking? Take up a new hobby in between potty training and nap time? Taz was about five years old at the time, and he'd seemed fairly musical, so I'd also asked my teacher to give him a few lessons in addition to teaching me.

But it was a disaster. The piano teacher was old-school, Russian, gifted, and passionate; she had no patience for little Taz, who was wild and silly. She wanted to pour her knowledge into an empty vessel; he wanted to play games. After two lessons, she basically fired herself as Taz's teacher, saying she couldn't work with him.

As she swept by my refrigerator on the way out the door, she noticed a photo I'd taped to the outside of the freezer that showed Taz at the beach.

In the image, he'd turned a pail upside down on the sand and was banging on it like a drum. He had a gleeful grin on his face, as if to say, "Yeah, I'm a wild little boy, makin' noise at the beach, woo-hoo!" To me it was the cutest picture in all the world. But Madame Tolstoya took one look at it and said, "You know, he's always up to something."

I stopped taking piano lessons myself a short time later after finding that the only time I could practice was 1 a.m., which my neighbors didn't appreciate, and which was a time of day when I was better off sleeping, anyway.

But hearing my friend talk about studying piano now that her son was nearly grown made me realize she was right. In a few years, I, too, would be free of most of the responsibilities of child rearing, and I could take up piano again if I cared to.

After all, I'd have to find something to do once I no longer had to supervise homework, sort mountains of laundry, and help everyone find obscure missing objects.

"Mom, do you know where my NBA Playoffs T-shirt is? You know, from that game Dad took me to a couple of years ago?"

"Mom, do you know where the Monopoly dice are? You know, the ones that fell on the floor when the board got knocked over the other day?"

"Mom, do you know where my flip-flops are? You know, the ones I took to the beach last year?"

"Mom, do you know where my math book is? You know, the one I brought home at the beginning of the semester?"

"Mom, do you know where my yearbook is? You know, the one from fifth grade?"

What am I, the Amazing Kreskin? What's really incredible is that, actually, I do know where all those things are, and ten thousand more like 'em. I dream of the day when I not only will not be asked to find all these objects, but my house will actually be free of them.

One year, Elon took the kids away on a road trip over spring break, and I spent the entire week throwing away things like one-armed action figures, toy cars with three wheels, and hundred-piece puzzles that only had eighty-nine pieces left. I stuffed them all in big bags and prayed that the garbage would be collected before they got home. If they didn't catch me getting rid of all this stuff, they'd never notice it was gone. But if they saw traces of it in the trash, I'd never be forgiven.

Thank goodness, the Department of Sanitation trucks rolled down the street the morning of the day they were due to arrive home. But I didn't count on one bag being left behind in one of the garbage cans.

They hadn't been back for ten minutes when Sport came to me in tears. "You threw away Zerg?" he wailed, clutching an eighteen-inch-tall plastic creature that once upon a time had bellowed in a deep and spooky electronic voice, "Who dares approach Zerg? Ya-ha-ha!" each time you pressed a button. Now it only moaned out vowels like a recording played at too slow a speed or a ghost from a phony seance: "Ooooh aaa-aah-oh orrrr?"

Taz wasn't crying, but he was mad—I'd thrown away his size-eight Jordans from three years earlier.

"Mom, I can't believe you did this—these are collector's items! Some day I'm going to sell these for a lot of money!" He held one in each hand and thrust them under my chin. They looked like a pair of used sneakers to me, but what did I know?

Taz and Sport scavenged a few other things out of the trash, alternating between anger at me for being so callous, and tenderness over the discovery of long-lost treasures. "Are you kidding me, I LOVE this!" was a typical exclamation upon finding a stained *Terminator* T-shirt that dated to the days when Ah-nold was merely a Hollywood actor instead of a governor.

Then they went back inside to unpack from their trip with Dad, showering me with a whole new collection of items they'd acquired on the road—like a key chain with a Sears Tower charm on it and a tote bag from the Splash Lagoon water park in western Pennsylvania— that no doubt I'd be trying to throw away the next time I did a big cleaning.

What can I say: I might be neurotic, but I'm not particularly sentimental—at least not about kitsch, souvenirs, and broken toys. OK, I admit, I did save a lock of blond curls from each of their first haircuts and the first baby tooth. And, as long as I'm baring my inner soul here, it's true, I saved that yucky thing that dries up and falls off from their umbilical cord. (Don't ask me why; I must be descended from witch doctors or something.)

And I'll probably be adding Taz's high school report cards to my small collections of memorabilia, too. His grades got a lot better as the year went on; one of his teachers said he was the poster boy for "most improved student of the year," and by the final report card, he had raised nearly all his Cs and Ds to Bs.

He'd even gotten an A, inexplicably, in biochemistry. When I told that to Linda, she said, "An A in biochemistry! Holy shit! I mean, if he's smoking something, it's obviously working for him!"

The best thing about the report card was that Taz said he wasn't happy with the fact that he'd gotten all those Bs. He vowed to work harder the next year to make As.

But the worst thing about the report card was that he

got one C, in the dreaded Español. Maybe I should have let him go on that trip to Cuba after all?

Besides, I'd told him I might let him go somewhere exciting sophomore year, provided he went out and got his working papers and a job over the summer. I suggested he try to secure a position in a coal mine, so that he could see what doing an honest day's work was really all about, but instead he managed to get hired as an assistant counselor at a local day camp.

It was fun to hear him complain about the children who didn't listen and how important it was to be firm with them and set limits, and how they take advantage if you don't. Ha! He didn't learn any of that from me.

It was also nice to hear him describe teaching a little boy how to roller-skate on a camp trip to a rink. And on a trip to an amusement park, he rode the big coaster with a camper who was scared. He won an award for counselor of the week, and told me he hoped he could work there again next summer.

But the best part was seeing him come home completely worn out every day.

"Oh my God," he'd groan, "I worked so hard today! I carried eighty-nine watermelons up three flights of stairs for a party! I played kickball in the park for seven hours straight! I went crazy looking for a kid who we thought was lost, but then we realized he was in the bathroom! It feels like all I do is work! I get up and go to work. I go to sleep, and then it's time to get up and go to work!"

Then he'd grin a gigantic grin.

"So, are you glad you took the job?" I asked.

"Oh yeah! It's really fun."

Sport, meanwhile, was going to sleepaway camp for two weeks—his first time, and mine. I never went to sleepaway camp as a child, and I felt very weepy while he was gone. I never sent Taz, either; he was happy just hanging out in the neighborhood when he was little.

But Sport was a serious jock and needed organized sports, morning, noon, and night—something that was hard to find in New York City, but that was easy to find in a camp. Still, I kept myself awake at night making lists of all the things that could happen to him: starvation, sunburn, bears, West Nile virus.

Then Linda reminded me that we knew all these girls from high school who were always talking about how much they loved sleepaway camp.

"Don't you remember, they talked about it so much that you just wanted to punch them?" she said.

It was true, I did remember that, and it cheered me up to think about it. Maybe Sport would love camp just like all those girls I'd known when I was a kid.

Indeed, when Sport finally did get home, it was clear he'd had a terrific time. He talked for an hour straight about all the fun things they did—jumping in the lake, archery, sleeping in the woods, s'mores.

And just like Linda had predicted, I kind of wanted to punch him. How dare he have such a good time without me?

Finally, I said, "Didn't anything bad happen at camp? Did you ever get in trouble for anything?

He looked at me ominously. "What happens in camp," he said, "stays in camp." He would say no more on the subject.

While Sport was away, I decided to take two weeks off from all household duties. I wasn't making dinner for anyone, or getting anyone a sandwich, or doing the laundry, or taking out the garbage. Within three days, the garbage was overflowing and we were out of toilet paper and milk.

And by the time Elon had done his third load of laundry, he was muttering under his breath that it was time Taz learned to do his Own Goddamn Laundry.

One night Elon and Taz spent ten minutes trying to figure out how to cook a Hot Pocket. I had made myself a beautiful salad, and I was washing it down with a nice tall glass of seltzer when I overheard their discussion.

"It says here to microwave it two to three minutes," Taz said. "Well, which is it? Two or three?"

"I don't know," said Elon, "but apparently we also need to use the crisping tray. What the heck is a crisping tray?"

One night while Sport was at camp, Taz took the train to his cousin's house on Long Island, where he planned to sleep over. It had been a long time since Elon and I had been alone together in our house, and we found ourselves at sixes and sevens. We hung around doing not much of anything, freaked the dog out by walking her together, which we never do, and decided around midnight that we were hungry. I hadn't made dinner, in keeping with my pledge, and Elon had decided that Hot Pockets were revolting.

We debated whether there was any place in our neighborhood open at that hour to eat. We had lived here for fifteen years, but we didn't know the answer, because we had never been out at midnight in all these years. We were always home with our kids.

We hopped in the car, drove down to the main drag in our neighborhood, where I usually see the CONY hanging out, and were astonished to see lots of places open at midnight, all filled with grown-ups—and no kids. We found a new burger place that we'd somehow missed the opening of. It was loud and fun and the food was fine.

We realized as we were eating that the dog had never been left home alone at this hour before; she must have be wondering what the hell was going on.

What's going on, Buddy, is that the kids are gone and we remembered how to have a life without them.

As long as we are still responsible for our children, we will take to heart the immortal words of Calvin Trillin, who is not exactly Dr. Spock or anything, but who wrote in a tribute to his late wife that they had agreed on a simple notion early on in raising their daughters:

"Your children are either the center of your life or they're not, and the rest is commentary."

But this rare night out was a preview of the day when they wouldn't be the center of our lives. They'd be gone and grown up. And then what?

Some friends with empty nests have gone back to school and started new careers as teachers and social workers, or gotten the master's and doctoral degrees they'd long dreamed of but hadn't had the energy to do when they were still running around to Little League games and PTA meetings.

A neighbor devoted herself to volunteering in a school in a poor neighborhood, and got everyone else on our block to donate their kids' used books to the library there. Another woman I know who still has a few more years of child rearing ahead of her fantasizes about just being a lazy bum—sitting in front of the TV every night without anybody asking her when's dinner or did you know we are out of paper towels. A lot of women I know get a puppy—I guess because they miss having something sweet and cuddly and messy to love.

The problem, I realized, was that for all the exhaustion and obsessions that come with being a mother, these two boys were about the most interesting thing that had ever happened to me. Even when they were driving me crazy, even when I wanted to kill Taz because of some dreadful thing he'd done, at least I was never saying, "What is the meaning of life? Why am I on this earth?" As long as there was a diaper to be changed or a meal to be cooked or a times table to be learned or a school trip to accompany, I had a purpose.

But now that Taz was fourteen, I could see more clearly that this purpose would eventually come to an end. Sure, I had a few more years ahead of me with Sport, but he was going to be fourteen before I knew it. And then what? Would I be trying to get the dog to play Monopoly with me?

In the meantime, if I'm feeling wistful for the days when Taz was younger, I can always call his cell phone. You see, with part of the money he earned at the day camp, he bought a new phone to replace the one that went in the toilet. He got his old number back, too, and even had his old message reconnected.

I'm glad, because now I can track him down when he's out chillin'. And if he chooses not to answer, that's OK, too. Because if he doesn't pick up, I get to hear that little squeaky voice from long ago on the message, and it reminds me of the days before he turned thirteen:

"Yo, whaddup, it's Taz!"

# Acknowledgments

Thanks to my family for letting me do this: to Elon and Linda for eagle-eye proofreading and honest feedback; and to many friends and colleagues for sharing stories and advice about raising adolescents.

Also, thanks to my editors and bosses at The Associated Press, for their encouragement in pursuing this project, and especially to Julie Rubin, for finding a home on the wire for the "Unjumpable Son" story that was the genesis of this book.

Finally, I am profoundly grateful to Jane Dystel, the most wonderful agent a writer could have, and to my editor at Crown, Rick Horgan, who helped me find the story inside the shtick.